SEX OFFENSES

AND THE MEN WHO COMMIT THEM

The Northeastern Series on Gender, Crime, and Law

EDITOR: Claire Renzetti

Recent books in this series

For a complete list of books in this series, please visit www.upne.com and www.upne.com/series/NGCL.html

SEX OFFENSES

AND THE MEN WHO COMMIT THEM

An Assessment of Sex Offenders on Probation

Michelle L. Meloy

Northeastern University Press
BOSTON

Published by University Press of New England
Hanover and London

Northeastern University Press

Published by University Press of New England,

One Court Street, Lebanon, NH 03766

www.upne.com

© 2006 by Northeastern University Press

Printed in the United States of America

5 4 3 2 1

Library of Congress Cataloging-in-Publication Data

Meloy, Michelle L.

Sex offenses and the men who commit them : an assessment of sex offenders on probation / Michelle L. Meloy.

   p.   cm. — (Northeastern series on gender, crime, and law)

Includes bibliographical references and index.

ISBN-13: 978-1-55553-653-4 (cloth : alk. paper)

ISBN-10: 1-55553-653-0 (cloth : alk. paper)

ISBN-13: 978-1-55553-654-1 (pbk.)

ISBN-10: 1-55553-654-9 (pbk.)

1. Sex crimes—United States.   2. Sex offenders—United States.

3. Criminal justice, Administration of—United States.   I. Title.

II. Series.

HV6561.M45   2006

364.15'32—dc22   2006001964

University Press of New England is a member of the Green Press Initiative. The paper used in this book meets their minimum requirements for recycled paper.

To my mother:

*For her unwavering support which made the
completion of this project possible.*

To my daughter:

*For sharing my time and attention with this book
in the first precious weeks of her life.*

To sex crime victims everywhere:

*It is my greatest wish that this work
will somehow contribute to fewer acts of
sexual violence.*

Contents

ACKNOWLEDGMENTS

I must begin by thanking the research participants who shared their thoughts and experiences with me on a topic that, most assuredly, was not comfortable to deal with honestly. Without them there would be no book. I am grateful to the Lake County, Illinois, probation department for hosting this research endeavor; my sincerest gratitude to directors Frank Kuzmickus and Scott Summers. I also acknowledge the special contributions of my mentors in academia and life, Ronet Bachman and Susan Miller. My sincere appreciation to Mary Fyvie-Poalelungi who provided her editorial assistance—and so much more. I would be remiss if I did not acknowledge the extraordinary research support of Shannon Paradise and the administrative assistance of Sherry Pisacano. I thank my department, my colleagues, and Rutgers University for providing the support and environment to pursue work like this. I would like to extend my sincere gratitude to those who reviewed all iterations of this work. Their insightful comments and suggestions vastly imported the strength and quality of this research. My deep appreciation to my editors, Claire Renzetti and Phyllis Deutsch, and University Press of New England for all their support and direction during this process. Finally, I thank my birth parents Georgia Scott and Arthur Meloy, my other excellent parents, Julian ("Scotty") and Dee, and the rest of my family—Anthony, Connor, Estralita, John, Laura, Mellina, baby Morgan, and Tara—for their support and patience through this process.

SEX OFFENSES

AND THE MEN WHO COMMIT THEM

Sex Offenders and Their Crimes

I told my daughter not to fear the boogyman because we
lived in a nice neighborhood where she would be safe. But
she wasn't. She was taken by a monster seeking only self-
gratification, a man driven by sick fantasies and pitiful needs.
—Brenda van Dam, in her victim impact statement,
about the male neighbor who raped and killed
her seven-year-old daughter, Danielle[1]

This book is one of the most comprehensive investigations to date on a group of convicted sex offenders and the legislation and criminal justice system that sanction, monitor and control their actions. The forthcoming chapters will introduce a plethora of topics and studies to enhance our understanding of sexual violence and the men who commit these crimes. This chapter details many introductory issues that set the stage for these later conversations such as the notion of sex offender "stranger-danger," why it is important to study sexual violence, the media's role in creating images of sex offenders, how these perceptions impact public policy, and many common myths about sex offenders. Additionally, this chapter describes how sex offenders are often punished by the criminal justice system and presents readers with their first glimpse into the original sex offender research that was the impetus for this book.

SEX OFFENDERS AND "STRANGER-DANGER"

Sex offenders are among the most despised and intriguing criminals of our time; indeed, this group incites more legislation than any other class of violent offenders. Numerous public policies have been directed toward sex offenders, both in the realm of tracking and controlling released offenders and in extending their removal from society. Yet, we know very little about these policies' public safety impact. The public's fascination and the media's overrepresentation of cases involving unknown or barely known assailants can easily result in misdirected fear and miscalculated risk. While it is appropriate to be horrified about sex crimes committed by strangers, it is equally inappropriate to ignore or minimize sexual violence perpetrated by a victim's spouse, partner, family member, date, friend, or acquaintance.

The term "stranger-danger" refers to the belief that unknown persons present the greatest risk for harm. For instance, women are taught to avoid being out alone at night as it is believed to place them at high risk of being assaulted by someone they do not know. Children are told never to talk with a stranger because he is the one who may hurt them. People who predominantly fear the statistically rare "stranger" attack may be more likely to support popular sex offender policies even though these policies probably cannot deliver their promises of increased safety. Actually, as we shall see in chapter 3, not only are these laws unlikely to enhance public safety they may actually exacerbate risks of victimization. If the goal of sex offender punishment is, first and foremost, to reduce sexual victimization then policies that prioritize retribution ("eye for an eye"), incapacitation ("lock them up and throw away the key"), or other punishment objectives like deterrence ("let this sentence be a warning") should be fully evaluated so we can determine their public safety impact. This book initiates this conversation.

WHY STUDY SEXUAL VIOLENCE?

The more that is understood about the risks associated with sexual offending and sexual victimization the more that can be done to prevent it. Several data sources are used to measure the extent to which sexual violence occurs in our country. The Uniform Crime Reports (UCR) is the most common source of arrest and conviction data. In addition to other crime categories, it collects information on two types of sex crimes: forcible rape (Part I offense) and "other sexual assaults" (Part II offense). One of the primary limitations with this data source, especially as it pertains to measuring sexual violence, is the long-standing problem of underreporting sex crimes to authorities. Research indicates that nearly 85 out of every 100 women who were sexually assaulted did not report their victimization to police (Kilpatrick, Edmunds, and Seymour 1992). This lack of reporting sex crimes to law enforcement officials means that the UCR is not the most valid measure of sexual violence. The National Incident-Based Reporting System (NIBRS) is a law enforcement–based data source designed to rectify many of the limitations suffered by the UCR.[2] One of the NIBRS' greatest strengths is that it allows police to include more detailed information regarding the crime(s), the offender(s), and the victim(s).

Given that sex crimes are often not reported to authorities, it is crucial that victimization data augment these official sexual violence statistics to present a more accurate picture of its prevalence and incidence in the United States. Some of the most widely used victimization data on sexual assault are the National Crime Victimization Survey (NCVS), the National Women's Study (NWS), the National Violence Against Women Survey (NVAWS), the National College Women Sexual Victimization Study, the Youth Risk Behavior Surveillance System (YRBSS), and the National Child Abuse and Neglect Data System (NCANDS). Victimization data sources uncover the especially "dark figure" of sex crime, reveal some of the reasons victims do not report their victimizations to authorities, and help unravel the physical, emotional, and financial costs associated with being a victim of a sex crime.

According to the Centers for Disease Control and Prevention (2004), sexual victimization has become a leading cause of injuries in this country. Conservative estimates indicate that 1 in 6 women and 1 in 33 men has been the victim of an attempted or completed rape (Tjaden and Thoennes 2000). These victimization rates climb even higher among some groups, such as individuals with disabilities (Marge 2003), college women (Fisher, Cullen, and Turner 2000), and young children (Snyder 2000). Moreover, recent studies indicate that more than two-thirds of all reported sexual assault victims were juveniles under the age of eighteen (Snyder 2000), with at least one in five girls and one in seven boys being the victim of sexual abuse before they reach their eighteenth birthday (Finkelhor 1994). Sexual abuse risks for children do not appear to be related to any particular ethnicity, race, socioeconomic class, or residential setting (La Fontaine 1990). There is some promising news, however, in that the year-to-year occurrence of child sexual victimization is currently on the decline in nearly every state (U.S. Department of Health and Human Services 2005). If this positive trend is sustainable, the prevalence of child sexual victimization in the United States will be reduced.

Sex crimes are notoriously problematic for victims because they are associated with a multitude of short- and long-term physical and emotional symptoms ranging from Rape Trauma Syndrome and death (by physical injury or suicide) to sexually transmitted diseases (Meadows 2001), psychosomatic disorders (Ullman 2004), chronic pain disorders (Koss and Heslet 1992), anxiety, depression, substance abuse (Meadows 2001), and an increased risk of sexual revictimization (Classen, Palesh, and Aggarwal 2005). Sexual assaults committed against persons who are physically challenged often result in physical incapacitation and extended periods of mandatory bed rest (Golding 1996). Children who are sexually abused often act out in sexually inappropriate ways, develop severe emotional and behavioral problems, have intense feelings of guilt and shame as a result of the abuse (according to the interview data, sex offenders failed to consider these feelings), and have a strong sense of betrayal by the offender (who is most often a close family member or friend). Furthermore, the children are left with a sense of abandonment and the belief that they are powerless to protect themselves and their bodies (Salter 1995).

The emotional toll is most severe for victims who know their offenders and most pronounced among victims who know their offenders well—the most common scenario. Therefore, when a sexual assault victim is familial, intimate, or psychologically connected with her abuser, her emotional wounds are more severe and her recovery longer and more complicated than for victims who are sexually assaulted by strangers.[3] One of the reasons for the increase in trauma between victims and offenders who are related or know one another is that the abuse is often more severe and can occur over a period of days, weeks, months, and even years; sexual assaults by strangers are often less physically intrusive and usually occur only one time (La Fontaine 1990). In spite of the increase in victim-related suffering associated with known assailants, and its more frequent occurrence, sexual assaults between strangers continues to be viewed as more serious by the media, criminal justice system, and the court of public opinion. There are some legitimate factors associated with the increased attention and response directed at stranger-related sex crimes. For example, sex crimes committed by unknown or barely known assailants are more likely to result in a victim's serious physical injury or death than sex offenses committed between victims and offenders who know one another (Greenfeld 1997). Also, recidivism data suggests that sex offenders who assault victims they do not know are at the greatest risk to recommit their crimes (Hanson and Bussiere 1998).

Given the epidemic proportion of sexual violence in our culture and the life-altering harm it can inflict on its victims and their families, enhancing our understanding of sex offenses and sex offenders is of the utmost importance.

THE MEDIA'S DEPICTION OF SEX CRIMES

The media highlights cases that are dramatic and sensational, which leads to an overrepresentation in news reports of stranger-related crimes. This stranger-danger presentation of violence persists despite the fact that strangers are involved in only a fraction of all sexual assaults. The likelihood of a child's being sexually assaulted by a stranger is the rarest victim-offender situation, occurring in only 7 percent of cases (Snyder 2000). This finding is shocking to media consumers, who can likely recall a string of high-profile child abductions and assaults, all involving stranger assailants or perpetrators that the victim barely knew. I shall discuss many of these infamous cases because they have had a profound impact on public policy and on how the law responds to sex offenders.

The highly publicized 1990 rape and sexual mutilation of a young Tacoma, Washington, boy by an unknown paroled male sex offender spurred the first sex offender community notification legislation.[4] The public was outraged that prior to his release from prison the assailant spoke of his continuing fantasies to kidnap, rape, and murder children. Washington's community notification laws received strong public support because it was believed that publicizing sex offender information would prevent victimizations.

Three years later, twelve-year-old Polly Klass, a blonde, blue-eyed girl was abducted from the bedroom window of her middle-class California home in the midst of a slumber party. The community response and intense media coverage of Polly's disappearance were unprecedented at the time. Thousands joined in the search for Polly and her disappearance became international news. The nationwide search for Polly continued for several weeks, until police made an arrest in the case and the killer led authorities to her body. A male ex-prisoner who had previously served time for child molestation was eventually convicted and sentenced to death for the kidnapping, rape, and murder of Polly.

In 1994, another child-victim/unknown-assailant case riveted the nation. This time it involved a seven-year-old Hamilton, New Jersey girl, named Megan Kanka. Like Polly, Megan was a pretty little girl from a white, middle-class neighborhood. She was raped and asphyxiated by her thirty-three-year-old neighbor, a paroled male child molester living with two other convicted sex offenders. According to police reports, Megan was lured into the home under the pretense of meeting the neighbor's new puppy. Once inside the house she was suffocated, raped, and later dumped in a nearby county park. Like the case in Washington State, the media coverage and a grassroots campaign to "do something" to stop dangerous child molesters were instrumental in the swift passage of New Jersey's sex offender registration and community notification requirement. New Jersey's sex offender law became the blueprint for similar legislation in all fifty states and the federal government.

In 1996 a nine-year-old girl, Amber Hagerman, was abducted outside her Arlington, Texas, neighborhood while riding her bicycle on a sunny Saturday afternoon. Neighbors reported hearing Amber scream and witnessed a man drag Amber off her bike and pull her into his truck before speeding away. The kidnapping riveted the local community and generated a tremendous amount of regional media attention. Four days after her disappearance, Amber's body was recovered from a drainage ditch only a short distance from her home. Her throat had been slashed. Interviews with neighbors provided police and the FBI with a description of the suspect and his vehicle. Although authorities searched extensively for the killer, the crime was never solved. The community responded to this kidnapping and murder by forming a partnership between law enforcement officials and area broadcasters. The AMBER (America's Missing: Broadcast Emergency Response) system was modeled after severe weather–warning alert systems: it repeats news bulletins, over the radio and across the television screen, about the abducted child and any details pertaining to the kidnapper's description and the type of vehicle used, requesting help from viewers.

The 2002 disappearance of Danielle van Dam, the gregarious, blonde, and blue-eyed young girl who was abducted from the bedroom of her California home in the middle of the night, also resulted in a media and law enforcement frenzy that culminated with an immediate arrest and the eventual recovery of young Danielle's body some fourteen days later. A male neighbor was eventually charged, convicted, and sentenced to death for her rape and murder. This tragic story touched America's heart, dominated the cable television airwaves for weeks, and became the impetus for a public plea to strengthen California's community notification law.

The stranger-abduction of Elizabeth Smart, the then fourteen-year-old, blonde, blue-eyed girl, snatched in darkness from the bedroom she shared

with her younger sister in the family's affluent neighborhood home dominated newspaper headlines and the twenty-four-hour cable networks for
weeks. The coverage of Elizabeth's kidnapping on the nationally syndicated
television program *America's Most Wanted* produced viewer tips that resulted in Elizabeth's rescue and the arrest of her apparent abductors.

Most recently, in unrelated incidents, two young white girls (nine-year-
old Jessica Lunsford and thirteen-year-old Sarah Lunde) were abducted
from their Florida homes and murdered. Each case resulted in the arrest
of a convicted sex offender. Jessica's disappearance from her Homosassa,
Florida, home generated national media attention and a massive search
that lasted for nearly three weeks until, on March 18, 2005, Jessica's
neighbor, a registered sex offender, admitted to sexually assaulting and
killing the child. Her body was recovered from a shallow grave, in the
backyard where the defendant was living, a short distance from Jessica's
home. Only a few weeks later, and a couple hundred miles away, an eerie
déjà vu was under way: the disappearance of Sarah Lunde. The national
media and hundreds of volunteers, including Jessica Lunsford's father, de-
scended on Ruskin, Florida, to help locate the young girl. One week later
her body was located in a small lake not far from her home. Sarah's mother
had once dated the convicted rapist who eventually confessed to choking
Sarah to death. The defendants in both of these cases are currently awaiting trial. The Florida legislature swiftly and unanimously passed the Jessica Lunsford Act, which requires a twenty-five-year minimum prison term
for offenders convicted of sexually assaulting a child under the age of
twelve and lifetime electronic surveillance, via global positioning technology, upon release from prison. A similar bill has been proposed in the
U.S. House of Representatives.

These cases share many of the same attributes: sensational and heart-
breaking stories representing statistically extraordinary occurrences (sex offenders who murder are the rarest type) (Browne and Lynch 1995; Pritchard
and Bagley 2001). These victimization stories feature completely innocent
and sympathetic victims often coupled with unknown or barely known
male assailants (many of whom were convicted of sex offenses in the past).[5]
The victims were white, physically attractive, under the age of eighteen.
Many of the victims came from families of middle and upper socioeconomic classes, and all but one victim was female. Previous research on
the criteria used to select cases for intensive media coverage reveals similar patterns (Meyers 1997; Meloy and Miller, in press). These biases
helps explain why some victimizations are selected for nationwide media

reporting while similarly situated ones are not. According to Milwaukee, Wisconsin, journalist Charlie Sykes, during the time period of Danielle and Elizabeth's kidnappings, families of color who possessed little social affluence yet were in the midst of the same personal crisis found it nearly impossible to summon media or police interest in the disappearance of their children. Apparently, the recipe for large-scale news coverage of sexual victimizations generally requires sensationalism accompanied by white, female victims (preferably a member of middle-class America) and an unknown or barely known assailant.

This type of news coverage reinforces the notion that only strangers are dangerous and that only young, white, female, middle- and upper-class victims are at risk of sexual violence. Today's lawmakers and judicial personnel have responded to these prevailing public perceptions of sexual victimization risk by enacting many legal policies targeted primarily at stranger offenders, including registration and community notification (often referred to as Megan's Law), AMBER alerts, intensive and/or lifetime probation (community supervision for life) and parole, specialized surveillance units, longer prison terms, and involuntary civil commitment (Hepburn and Griffin 2004; Kruttschnitt, Uggen, and Shelton 2000). A comprehensive discussion of how victim-offender relationships impact sex offender laws will be discussed in chapter 3; for now it is important to note that the relationship exists and that the images and perceptions of risk can result in the creation of criminal justice policies even when the beliefs are based on misconceptions.

COMMUNITY-BASED SANCTIONS FOR SEX OFFENDERS

A recent trend in the criminal justice response to sex crimes, and hence the focus of this book, is the increased reliance on community-based sanctions for monitoring sex offenders (Center for Sex Offender Management 2002). Sex offenders are being sentenced to probation and parole in record numbers (Greenfeld 1997), for increasingly long periods of time, and under more stringent conditions than ever before. Shrinking state budgets, prison overcrowding, advanced community supervision technologies and techniques, improvements in therapeutic and pharmacological interventions, and the possibility of community supervision for life (currently an option in three states) account for much of the increase of sex offenders on probation and parole.

The criminal justice system has responded to this sentencing change in a number of ways. Eighty-five percent of the nation's probation and parole departments have implemented special conditions for offenders convicted of sex crimes (English et al. 1996; Lane Council of Governments 2003), with more and more departments offering specialized caseloads and specially trained officers to supervise sex offenders (Center for Sex Offender Management 2002). At first glance, supervising sex offenders in the community sounds a risky business. Many experts believe, however, that collaborative, multidisciplinary approaches to community-based sex offender management and treatment offer the greatest promise to reduce recidivism (Center for Sex Offender Management 2001 and 2002).

This argument is supported, in part, by the body of research that suggests that sex offenders who successfully complete treatment recidivate less often and less quickly than their untreated counterparts (Alexander 1999; Hanson 2000; Mailloux et al. 2003; Marshall, Anderson, and Fernandez 1999).[6] The definition of "success" in treatment varies somewhat from one treatment provider to the next. The clinicians treating the sex offenders involved in this particular study developed a set of criteria each offender must meet to be considered successfully "graduated" from sex offender treatment. For instance, a level system is used to designate progress in therapy and offenders must master the top level to earn a successful discharge from treatment. The completion of workbook exercises and the passing of a polygraph examination are also standard treatment completion requirements. Extant literature indicates similar criteria are commonly used by forensic experts who specialize in sex offender therapy. The efficacy of therapeutic intervention for some sex offender populations—combined with the fact that nearly 75 percent of all sex offenders sentenced to prison do not receive treatment during their incarceration (Turner, Bingham and Andrasik 2000)—means that mandating it as part of community supervision may be the best method to ensure that sex offenders receive the direction necessary to help control their violent behavior.

Let me provide an example to illustrate my point. The Bureau of Justice Statistics (2003) published a report on prisoner releases indicating that in a single year approximately 14,683 felony sex offenders walked out of state prisons in the United States (Langan, Schmitt, and Durose 2003). If 75 percent of these inmates did not receive therapy during their prison stay, then more than eleven thousand untreated sex offenders were released back into the community that year alone.[7] Because on the whole, untreated sex offenders are more likely to reoffend than successfully treated offenders, and to do so more quickly and more often, releasing untreated and unsupervised sex offenders back into the community is not in the best interest of public safety. The rehabilitation mandate and close supervision by probation and parole agents that is now commonplace among community-based sentences (that is, requirement of successful performance in treatment and compliance with other court orders such as behavioral restrictions on risky behavior) may help explain why the three-year follow-up recidivism rate of a national sample of felony sex offenders sentenced to probation (in lieu of prison) is *lower* than that of a national sample of felony sex offenders sentenced directly to prison (Meloy 2005). Overall, specialized and intensive community-based supervision for sex offenders is a fraction of the cost of long-term incarceration and may be safer for communities than prison sentences that do not offer, encourage, or mandate treatment success and community reintegration strategies (Center for Sex Offender Management 2001; English et al. 1996).[8]

SEX OFFENDERS: FACT OR FICTION?

Throughout this book much of what we were taught to believe about sex offender risk, by the media and commonsense wisdom, will be challenged by scientific findings that are often in conflict with public perceptions on the issue. For example, most sex offenders know their victims. If you are a young child (under the age of six) who was sexually victimized, 97 percent of the time, your abuser was a family member or an acquaintance (Snyder 2000). Similarly, if you are a female college student you are much more likely to be sexually assaulted in your own dorm room or apartment and by your own date or classmate than you are in an outside location or by an unknown person (Fisher, Cullen, and Turner 2000). Sadly, female college students continue to be more afraid that they will be victimized by strangers while walking across campus at night or leaving a bar alone than they are of the most likely sexual assaults, which involve personal residences and personal relationships (Fisher and Sloan 2003). This misperception of victimization risk unnecessarily restricts women's movement and life choices and results in miscalculations of potential harm.

Another commonly held misconception—often reinforced by the media and public officials alike—is that sex offenders are more dangerous than other violent criminals because they inevitably recommit their crimes and cannot be successfully treated or rehabilitated. The issue of recidivism and recidivism rates and treatment success for different types of sex offenders will be more fully explored in chapter 2. Suffice it to say here, the perception of increased and inevitable dangerousness and re-offense is not true. In the most simplistic of comparisons (sex offenders versus other serious criminals), recidivism rates are significantly lower among men who sexually offend than among other types of serious and violent criminals. Specifically, sex offenders released from prison had lower rearrest rates than armed robbers, kidnappers, and individuals incarcerated for serious assaults, as well as other types of offenders (Langan and Levin 2002). As a matter of fact, in this national study of released prisoners, murderers, rapists, and other sexual assault offenders had the lowest re-arrest rates of all the serious offenders released from prison (Langan and Levin 2002, 8). Also, it is commonly assumed that most sex offenders do not respond to therapy. While this seems to be true for some groups of sex offenders (especially pedophiles and other seriously deviant offenders) it is not a unilateral reality. Situational child molesters (not to be confused with pedophiles, who have a severe psychological diagnosis punctuated by a sexual fixation on children), incest offenders, and male rapists of adult women have responded positively to cognitive behavioral modification treatment techniques.

There is an overriding belief that the general and specific deterrent impacts of sex offender legislation will outweigh any antitherapeutic or unanticipated consequences resulting from the laws. If sex offender registration and community notification result in offenders feeling alienated from family and friends or in their having difficulty maintaining stable employment or residency, it is believed to be "worth it" from a public safety perspective because these measures promise to reduce sexual violence and protect victims. These well-intentioned policies, however, may actually *increase* the likelihood that convicted sex offenders will recommit sex crimes, in part, because important desistance variables such as community reintegration, stress management, and lifestyle stability are interrupted by sex offender legislation (Zevitz 2004). Effective intervention strategies must take into account the typical victim-offender relationship, differences in sex offending populations and risk, and predictors of sexual violence and desistance. In other words, they should be grounded in science and offer realistic possibilities for deterrence and increased public safety. This study provides answers to important questions by dissecting the performance of sex offenders on probation in terms of their sexual recidivism rate, the high-risk factors associated with failure during probation, and the offenders' thoughts about the criminal justice system and what they believe to be the motivations and causes behind their own sexually deviant behavior.

This investigation involved a group of convicted adult male sex offenders who were on probation during 2000 and 2001 in a Midwestern city in the United States. Trained probation officers within a specialized unit supervise all convicted sex offenders serving a term of community-based supervision in this jurisdiction. These men had been arrested and convicted of sexually assaulting family members, partners and ex-partners, dates, children in their neighborhood, acquaintances, and strangers. Some of the men were also on probation for voyeurism, indecent exposure, and possession of child pornography.[9] Court files, probation records, arrest documents, and clinical reports were used to gather information about their sociodemographic characteristics, descriptions of their crimes and criminal history, the conditions of their community supervision, their treatment status and protocol, their recidivism rate, and the factors predictive of probation failure. In addition, I conducted interviews, on a voluntary basis, with a subsample of the probationers and asked them questions pertaining to their victims, themselves, their perceptions of what caused them to act out in a sexually deviant and criminal fashion, and what they thought about their criminal justice, probation, and mandatory treatment experience. Finally, the men spoke of their justifications, motivations, and rationalizations for committing sex crimes.

A detailed description of the entire sample will be provided in chapter 4, but there are a few general statements to be made here. Of the 169 men included in the study, the average age was thirty-four years old. Most of the men were white and not married at the time of their offense. The vast majority of the offenders in this specialized probation unit committed sex crimes against a family member or friend. This victim-offender relationship is the most common among sex crimes and is often viewed as less serious than crimes committed by strangers—which may have contributed to the offenders receiving probation instead of a prison sentence. Sex criminals who are sentenced to prison are more likely to have victimized someone they did not know (Greenfeld 1997).

This study has three primary research objectives: (1) to determine the extent to which convicted male sex offenders recidivate while on community-based supervision; (2) to identify the high-risk factors associated with their sexual recidivism during probation; and (3) to test deterrence and rational choice theories as a way to understand the committing of sex crimes. To capture the complex issues, triangulated research methods are used (Denzin 1997). Triangulation allows multiple methods to study a phenomenon simultaneously. The combination of qualitative and quantitative methods allows for a more comprehensive probe into sexual recidivism. Qualitative methods are particularly useful when studying relatively unexplored topics or when substantive knowledge in an area is limited (Strauss and Corbin 1998; Lofland and Lofland 1995): precisely the case here as only a handful of studies investigate sex offender performance on probation. For example, because empirical data are lacking on the psychological processes of sex offender decision-making, qualitative research may glean insight that would not surface through the use of other types of research methods. Although qualitative methods add depth and richness to the data and recognize themes or patterns that may not emerge through statistical techniques, these designs cannot explain how factors interact with one another or identify which measures have the most significant influence on sexual recidivism. Therefore, quantitative research is necessary to accomplish these tasks. Because both quantitative and qualitative methodologies have their own specific strengths, they can complement one another and strengthen the end project. In sum, the use of multiple methods helps to overcome inherent biases that exist when relying exclusively on any one methodology. In addition, triangulation increases the validity and reliability of findings through a more complete analysis of the data.

Because males constitute 96 percent of the offenders in reported sexual assaults (Snyder 2000), my investigation will be limited to men. I do not mean, of course, that female sex offenders do not exist or that their crimes are less severe. As a matter of fact, when women do commit sex crimes they are likely to offend against the very youngest and most helpless victims, children under the age of six: women account for 12 percent of all offenses against this age group (Snyder 2000). However, because the motivations and causes of female-perpetrated sexual violence are believed to be different than male-on-female acts of sexual violence, they will not be discussed in this book.

DETERRENCE AND RATIONAL CHOICE

Sex-offending behavior is generally attributed to a mental illness or psychopathology often associated with irresistible impulses; as such, it has been studied predominantly from a medical perspective. In other words, sex offenders are typically seen as men ruled by sexually aggressive tendencies that render them powerless to overcome these urges, thereby making it impossible for potential offenders to engage in a rational assessment of potential pleasures or pains associated with their actions (Bachman et al. 1992). The present study suggests something completely contrary: namely, that sex offenders are rational, calculating beings who expend time and energy in the planning stages of their sexual criminality. Evidence suggests that most rapists of adult women do not commit their crimes due to "irresistible impulses" but that they carefully and thoughtfully plan their crimes (Haas and Haas 1990; Pithers 1990; Quinsey and Earls 1990; Warren, Reboussin, and Hazelwood 1998). This study uses the criminological theories of deterrence and rational choice to test this premise. Because one of the primary objectives of the Western criminal justice system is to deter criminal acts, deterrence is notably one of the most fascinating and heavily researched theoretical concepts in criminology—yet it rarely has been tested on sex offenders.

Deterrence and rational choice theories assume that individual decision-making stems from rational consideration of the benefits (pleasure) and the risks (pain) associated with an act. In other words, individuals make a rational choice to obey or break the law based on their internal calculation of the potential pleasure or pain associated with the crime. According to this cost-benefit analysis of offending, individuals decide against committing a sex crime if they believe the penalty would outweigh the potential pleasure associated with the behavior. Theoretically, such an assessment relies on the offenders' own personal experiences with the criminal justice system, their overall perceptions of legal sanctions, and their knowledge of punishment received by similarly situated offenders. If one offender received a sanction for rape that was seen as "getting off easy," a potential offender may determine that the anticipated pleasure exceeds the anticipated pain for engaging in a similar act. For a cost-benefit analysis of crime to benefit society, punishment must be severe enough, certain enough, and swift enough to deter criminal behavior.

Because of the overall popularity of deterrence in our criminal justice system, it has shaped many sex offender laws. This theory has two different goals: *specific* and *general* deterrence. Specific deterrence sex offender policies are geared directly toward the *convicted* individual and are successful to the extent they deter him/her from committing additional sex crimes. General deterrence sex offender laws, on the other hand, are aimed at *potential* offenders and are determined to be successful when would-be offenders are dissuaded from engaging in illegal sex acts as a result of the punishment received by convicted sex offenders. Involuntary civil commitment, registration and community notification, lengthy prison terms, lifetime probation and parole (community supervision for life)—all exemplify components of both specific and general deterrence by implying that sex offenders avoid committing sex acts because the social costs are too high.

Early deterrent studies were designed to consider only macrolevel effects (actual arrest data and sentence severity) and ignored the microlevel factors (psychological processes) that are part of the decision-making process to commit an illegal act. In other words, the *objective* reality of legal sanctions (in terms of certainty, severity, and swiftness of punishment) and the *perceived* reality of legal sanctions (what the offender believes will happen in terms of certainty, severity, and swiftness of punishment) could be incongruent, which would result in a miscalculation of risk. In fact, research suggests that perceptions of formal legal sanctions often do *not* match their objective reality and that perception of costs and benefits for engaging in crime seldom remain constant over time.[10] Therefore, researchers began to account for these perceptions of legal sanctions (for example, asking respondents to assess the likelihood of arrest and punishment given certain situations) when testing utility-based explanations for crime.

Although perceptual studies were more effective at capturing part of the psychological processes associated with deterrence, they still failed to give equal time and attention to the perceptions of the positive side of the deterrence equation (that is, assessments of potential gains and pleasures associated with committing the act). A further limitation with initial perceptual studies is that they suffered from temporal order problems: *prior* criminal behavior was examined against *present* perceptions of the certainty of arrest and the severity and swiftness of punishments. Temporal order problems were eventually resolved through a design structure (surveys and vignettes depicting hypothetical contexts and situations) that allowed for an immediate effect (instead of the lagged response that previously existed) of perceptions of risk on projections of future behavior. A similar technique was attempted in this research. Unfortunately, because only one of the respondents indicated that he would be willing to commit another sex offense, it was impossible to conduct any meaningful analysis.

There remained other problems with traditional deterrence research. For instance, it did not take into account the role of moral inhibitions or the extent of social disapproval associated with an act. Such extralegal factors may be acutely relevant to sex crimes because, according to conventional definitions, they are immoral acts. In essence, it may not be the severity, swiftness, or certainty of legal sanctions that dissuades an offender from committing a crime but rather his/her belief that it is simply immoral or wrong to do so (Williams and Hawkins 1986). In actuality, many studies did find that the relationship between extralegal factors and deterrence is statistically stronger and more significant than the correlation between deterrence and formal legal sanctions.

One of the more recent advancements in studying deterrence is the inclusion of rational choice theory.[11] Rational choice theory includes such extralegal factors in its analyses as low self-control, feelings of shame, embarrassment or remorse, internal moral inhibitors, threat of formal punishments, and the pleasure associated with offending.[12] According to a rational choice perspective, opportunity, situational factors and the environment, victim or target, and the offenders' perception of the likelihood of apprehension influence the pleasure versus pain calculation (Cornish and Clarke 1986). These informal social control variables permit a more balanced critique of the subjective costs and benefits associated with crime.

Using this broader perspective on cost-benefit analysis, the offender's assessment of whether to commit a crime is dependent upon the situational context of the incident and the type of crime considered. To illustrate, an offender may assess that the opportunity and victim are "right" for committing a sex offense (say, for instance, that the potential offender's adolescent niece is staying with him and his wife) but the situational context may not be "right" (the potential offender's wife is nearby and therefore he deems the chances of detection as high). As a result, the potential offender decides not to commit the sex crime. As this example illustrates, rational choice perspective takes the focus away from structural theories of crime and deviance and instead concentrates primarily on event-based explanations of criminality (O'Grady, Asbridge, and Abernathy 2000). Attention to the specifics surrounding a particular criminal incident can help explain why a certain offender at a particular point in time made the choice to commit or not to commit a criminal act.

It has been argued that because the expected utility of a specific behavior is unique to different crimes, a "crime specific focus is necessary because the costs and benefits of one crime may be quite different from those of another" (Piquero and Tibbetts 1996, 482). This argument suggests the perceptions of risks versus pleasures of offending should be examined separately for different types of offenses, thus lending support to studying deterrence and rational choice explanations of offending on populations of sex offenders. Moreover, research indicates that some forms of sexual violence may be best understood using a rational choice framework because they are indeed deliberate and calculated actions (Nagin and Paternoster 1993; Bachman et al. 1992; Marshall and Barbaree 1990). For instance, research on rapists' decision-making reveals that many rapes are planned events, not spur-of-the-moment decisions (Haas and Haas 1990). In another study, serial rapists indicated that they often traveled some distance to locate their victim and that many of the rapists followed predeveloped scripts when they raped women (Warren, Reboussin, and Hazelwood 1998). They exerted much control over whom they victimized, how they did it, and when they would commit the rape.

One of rational choice theory's greatest strengths is that it corrects for the imbalance of other utility-based explanations of offending that failed to consider fully the subjective benefits or pleasures that offenders may experience when committing their crimes. For example, findings indicate that potential pleasure derived from the act can be the *most* important criterion in the defendants' assessment of whether or not to offend (Nagin and Paternoster 1993; Piliavin et al. 1986). This more comprehensive estimation of costs and benefits (from an offender's perspective) may go a long way in explaining why rational choice models have garnered stronger empirical support than earlier deterrence studies (see Bachman et al. 1992; Grasmick and Bursik 1990; Klepper and Nagin 1989; Nagin and Paternoster 1993; Piquero and Tibbetts 1996). The hope, of course, is that these new models will lead to new insights into the psychological process of deterrence and therefore teach us how best to control and deter violent offenders.

Deterrence and rational choice theories ground this research in at least two important ways. First, data collected from probation files is one way for the deterrent impact of formal legal sanctions to be tested. According to the theory, sex offenders who receive the most severe sanctions (high cost) will be less likely to commit a new sex offense while on probation compared with the sex offenders who had fewer restrictions and requirements (lower cost) levied to their community-based supervision. Second, interviews were conducted, with the men who agreed, to obtain their perspectives on countless issues pertaining to sexual violence and to hear directly from them about their experiences with the criminal justice system and its direct (and indirect) impact upon their immediate and future behavior.[13] Contextually, what is different from past attempts to explore the relationship between deterrence/rational choice ideologies and sexual violence (Bachman et al. 1992) is the use of convicted sex offenders rather than samples of convenience or of offenders convicted of crimes other than sex offenses. This is the first time that deterrence and rational choice theories have been tested in this way.

The subsequent chapters discuss many issues relevant to sexual violence. Chapter 2 examines the clinical data on sex offenders. It explores what is known about sex offender recidivism (the science of predicting which sex offenders are most likely to sexually reoffend) and the data on the effectiveness of treatment for sex offenders. Chapter 3 focuses on the legislative warfare that is waged against sex offenders: mandatory prison terms, involuntary civil commitment, sex offender registration and community notification, AMBER alerts, mandatory treatment and lifetime probation and parole (community supervision for life). This chapter also tackles the difficult questions of the ultimate impact these legal reforms are likely to have on community safety and reducing sexual violence. Chapter 4 provides a comprehensive description of the sample characteristics and summarizes the significant statistical research findings associated with the study (that is, sex offender recidivism while on probation and its predictive factors). Chapter 5 highlights the interview data conducted on a subsample of the convicted sex offenders. The men spoke about themselves and their victims and gave reasons why they committed their sex crimes. Chapter 6 concludes with a summary of the major research findings and suggests how these results, in conjunction with other research and legal analysis, can guide policymakers, practitioners, and researchers toward an empirically based public policy response to sex offending that offers real promise in terms of deterrence and increased protection from sex offenders.

Studying Sexual Violence

Child molesters, angry rapists, predators of all sorts only show
the face they want you to see, when they want you to see it.

—Salter 2003, 50

As indicated in chapter 1, empirical research on sex offenders is predominantly medical or psychologically oriented; thus sexual violence is examined almost exclusively as an illness or severe abnormality. This monolithic approach to studying sex crimes has significantly restricted investigations dealing with diagnosis, illness, and rehabilitation. It has also limited other types of theoretical rationales for understanding sexual violence—such as whether sex offenders are rational calculating beings. Driven in part by public pressure to "do something" about sex offenders and their crimes, a great deal of work has focused on the issue of sexual recidivism and the related topics of identifying high-risk offenders (those most likely to recidivate) and the effectiveness of therapy for this diverse offending population. In this chapter I grapple with many of these important issues.

RECIDIVISM AMONG SEX OFFENDER POPULATIONS

Because of the devastating effects of sexual victimization, the most important goal of the criminal justice system must be to eliminate recidivism. Therefore, the extent to which sex offenders recommit their crimes is a critical public policy issue. Unfortunately, researchers are unable to provide a clear, definitive answer regarding the true extent of recidivism. Differences in the way recidivism is defined (sex offenses only, any new crime, or technical violations while on probation or parole), measured (self-report, arrest, conviction, incarceration), length of follow-up period (opportunity to offend), and the methodological design of the study result in disparate recidivism outcomes from study to study.[1] Moreover, recidivism studies of sexual violence suffer from difficulties such as low base rate,[2] heterogeneity of the population (prison- or community-based and the types of sex offenders included), and underreporting problems atypical of other crimes.

The lack of official reporting of sex crimes is partly attributed to the fact that victims of sexual violence often experience denial, fear, shame, and embarrassment—all of which result in a reluctance to notify police. Another contributing factor to the "dark figure" of sexual violence is that sex offenders rarely, if ever, freely disclose their criminal sex acts. Victimization studies (see chapter 1), directed interviews between offenders and forensic experts, and polygraph data on sex offenders (Salter 2003) indicate that sex offenders commit many more sex crimes than official statistics suggest. For instance, one of the men included in this study was convicted of luring a ten-year old female into his car and forcibly fondling her breasts and genitals (under her clothing) before he released her in front of her school a short time later. At the time of sentencing, the court was not aware that there were other sexual victimizations in the offender's criminal past. The fact that he molested five young boys years earlier (he was a family friend) was only revealed as a result of a probation-mandated sex offender evaluation and polygraph examination. These additional victimizations were not available in official arrest records because the man had never been questioned or charged for these other sex crimes; nor had he admitted to committing them until he was forced to take a polygraph examination. Underreporting by male victims of sexual assault is believed to be even more pronounced than it is among females. It is likely that the boys were too embarrassed or frightened to report what happened to them.

Good starting points for investigating the efficacy of sentencing sex offenders to probation are (1) to examine their failure (new sex crimes) during and after probation and (2) to look at the rates of recidivism for sex offenders who receive criminal punishments other than probation. Although a direct deterrent comparison between various sentencing options is not appropriate in the absence of a random assignment to one sanction (prison) or the other (probation), it is still helpful to review what is known about the recidivistic behavior of sex offenders sentenced directly to probation as well as the recidivism of sex offenders released from prison. As it is assumed that offenders sent to prison are the most serious and dangerous criminals, it is not surprising that recidivism rates for released sex offenders appear higher than for other sanctioned sex offending populations. A national and oft-cited study found that the general (nonsexual) rearrest rate among sex offenders released from numerous state prisons was 43 percent and the sexual rearrest rate was 5 percent, for a three-year follow-up period (Langan, Schmitt, and Durose 2003). Rearrest rates (for both sexual and nonsexual offenses) among sex offender probationers indicate they reoffend no more often than sex offenders released from prison and that they may actually recidivate less than released prisoners even when they are observed for longer follow-up periods (Hepburn and Griffin 2004; Kruttschnitt, Uggen, and Shelton 2000; Meloy 2005).

One of the few studies to date to investigate the performance of sex offenders on probation found a 35 percent rearrest rate for general (nonsexual) offenses and a 5.6 percent rearrest rate for additional sex crimes, during a nearly five-year follow-up period (Kruttschnitt, Uggen, and Shelton 2000). One of the only studies to investigate the recidivism of a nationwide sample of felony sex offender probationers found that within thirty-two different jurisdictions across seventeen states, only 4.5 percent of the sex offender population committed a new sex crime within three years of being placed on probation (Meloy 2005). Both of these studies cite recidivism averages below the failure rate for released sex offenders who were sent to prison instead of probation. The sexual recidivism rate for the sex offender population studied here was 12 percent. The broad operational definition of recidivism used in this study—any indication of additional sexually criminal behavior, irrespective of whether it resulted in a new arrest—and the breadth of sources available for review of recidivistic activity (criminal record checks, clinical and probation files, surveillance officer notes, and polygraph results) allowed for a more comprehensive assessment of recidivism than is typical in most studies.

As mentioned earlier, many factors contribute to the variability in outcomes across recidivism research. Subsamples of sex offenders have a recorded recidivism rate at about 10 percent after a fifteen-year follow-up time frame; in contrast, other subsamples (slightly more than 10 percent) of sex offenders have recidivism rates upward of 40 percent (Hanson and Thornton 2000). Key factors associated with high or low recidivism rates for sex offenders: type of sex offender, prior sex offense history, the presence or absence of violence as part of the sex crime, the victim-offender relationship, the victim's age and gender, and the demographics of the population under investigation (for example, age of the sex offender or whether he is a released prisoner). Because of the complications associated with sex offender recidivism research, longitudinal designs are needed, as are populations that can be differentiated by sanctioning option or offending behavior.[3]

We have begun to see that sex offender recidivism rates can be very different. Rapists (of adult women) typically have the highest recidivism rates, hovering around 40 percent. Heterosexual intrafamilial child molesters have the lowest rate of reoffense, usually around 3 percent. These official (or known) rates show a group of sex offenders with different risks to reoffend. Although most child molesters (excluding pedophiles)[4] have lower reoffense rates than rapists of adult women, both categories of criminals share a common victim-offender relationship: by a vast majority, they know their victims. Sexual assaults between victims and offenders who know each other are one of the most consistent findings in the sexual violence literature. As a matter of fact, the youngest of victims (children under age six) are molested by a stranger in only 3 percent of known cases (Snyder 2000). All the other instances of child molestation occur by a family member, friend, or acquaintance to the child. However rare stranger-assailants are, they are dangerous and high-risk sex offenders and their crimes should be taken very seriously.

Given that women and children are more likely to be victimized sexually (and in other ways as well) by family members and friends than by strangers, a well-informed social policy agenda targeting acquaintance situations would likely prove more beneficial to reducing recidivism than current sex offender laws, which focus almost exclusively on (statistically rare) stranger-assailants of children. The existing research on chronic sexual violence does not adequately address whether current sex offender legislation and criminal justice practices are a deterrent to sex offenders. Because a utility-based explanation of crime is beyond the traditional purview of the medical community, achieving deterrence is discussed in terms of accurate clinical assessments, correcting cognitive distortions, eliminating criminal sexual fixation, and treatment intervention.

PREDICTION OF DANGEROUSNESS

Identification of serious offenders is one of the most crucial and difficult objectives of criminal justice officials and forensic clinicians. Assessments of future risk and dangerousness impact pretrial release, sentencing options, postsentencing (parole), community notification and tiering levels, and treatment amenability and protocol. As with other areas related to sex offenders, the majority of research on sexual violence risk appraisal has been conducted by the medical community (Alexander 1999; Furby, Blackshaw, and Weinrott 1989; Hanson 2000a and b; Mailloux et al. 2003; Marshall, Anderson, and Fernandez 1999). Inevitably, clinical (diagnosis) and psychological areas (emotional trauma or distress) have received more attention than situational (loss of employment, housing, significant relationships) or criminal justice–related measures (prison, community supervision, registration, and community notification).

There are two types of risk assessment: clinical and actuarial. Forensic clinical judgments are grounded in professional training, clinical experience with the population, and first hand knowledge of the individual being assessed. In contrast, actuarial measures of risk consist of statistical predictions based on how others have responded in a similar situation or on an offender's similarity to the group. Actuarial predictions of future dangerousness consist of statistical models and risk factor instruments. Historically, assessments of future violence were based only on the (often inaccurate) perceptions of an individual evaluator and were plagued by problems of overprediction of dangerousness. Because of recent advancements in statistical predictive measurements, actuarial predictors of future dangerousness are more precise than clinical assessments (Harris, Rice, and Quinsey 1993; Mossman 1994; Rice 1997). Therefore, they are becoming the preferred risk assessment tool and are used exclusively or in conjunction with clinical impressions.

Despite improvements in the science of actuarial risk prediction, limitations and errors persist. For instance, actuarial evaluations are often conducted on global samples of "sex offenders" with no delineation made for offending behavior characteristics (Prentky, Lee, Knight, and Cerce 1997). This global population phenomenon occurs in recidivism research also and is problematic in both areas because child molesters, rapists, and intra/extrafamilial sex offenders can have dramatically different rates of recidivism. Therefore, dangerousness prediction research that assumes sex offenders to be a homogeneous group will inevitably experience errors: the risk of dangerous offenders will be masked while the predictions for lower-risk offenders will be statistically inflated.

A major impediment in the risk appraisal of sex offenders is the overreliance on static (nonchanging) risk factors. Many static factors (for example, history of psychological trauma, severe personality disorder diagnosis, prior sex offenses, or arrests for other crimes) are long-term indicators of violent behavior. Static (unchanging) factors can identify characteristics associated with recidivism at some point in the future but they cannot discern *when* an offender is likely to recidivate. Neither can they measure changes in an offender's risk situation; such measurement would require information about dynamic (changeable/fluid) features in the offender's life. Situational risk factors likely to create a shift in an offender's dangerousness include residential/housing issues, change in employment status, significant relationship issues, treatment intervention, intoxication status, and sexual arousal. Stated another way, situational shifts in an offender's life may increase or decrease his short-term risk or likelihood of sexually reoffending. Obviously, the ability to assess instantaneous changes in a sex offender's level of risk would be a tremendous asset in enhancing the effectiveness of community-based sanctions.

Research, however, has overwhelmingly concentrated on correlates of long-term propensities of reoffense (static) over immediate assessments of risk (dynamic). Surely, part of the reason for this imbalance is because static factors are easier to study: they involve information that is more accessible (official records and reports), and they do not change over time. It is much more difficult constantly to measure and track changes in an offender's housing status, his impulse control, his intoxication status, and how well he is responding to treatment or cooperating with probation. Nevertheless, gauging these situational variables is certainly worth the difficulty and should be a mandated part of decisions to release an offender from custody or place him on probation.

Another reason that static factors have been prioritized is that they designate high-risk offenders (using historical/unchanging data) and provide few opportunities for an offender's risk level to be dropped: they don't measure situational events that may reduce risk (stable employment; living arrangements that are constant, supportive, and appropriate; treatment success; compliance with probation; and so forth). Considering the societal and political concerns about some sexual assaults, it is not surprising that evaluators such as judges, probation officers, forensic therapists, and parole board members embrace a conservative policy when making appraisals of risk. *Over*estimating an offender's potential for future violence (false positive) is viewed as far less egregious than *under*estimating a defendant's degree of dangerousness (false negative). Among the greatest fears of criminal justice practitioners is that a sex offender will reoffend while under their supervision.

An additional obstacle in assessing a sex offender's level of risk is the lack of data on what actually predicts chronic sexual violence. Research is lacking on how to identify which sex offenders pose the greatest risk of committing additional acts of sexual violence. Correlates used to predict general criminal recidivism and nonsexual violent behavior are often not statistically significant predictors of chronic sexual violence (Hanson and Bussiere 1998; Meloy 2005; Rice and Harris 1997). Actuarial risks of dangerousness for sex offenders need to be specific to the population; therefore, evaluators need to be explicit in terms of the type of behavior the models purport to predict by differentiating between assessments for general recidivism/violence and sexual recidivism/violence (Hanson 1998).

To recap, significant inroads have been made in the prediction of dangerousness. It was not long ago when accurate assessments of future harm were believed to be more voodoo than science. Improvements in statistical techniques and model specification have allowed researchers to assess more accurately which violent offenders are most likely to recidivate, at least in the long term. There is still work to be done, however; more research is needed on dynamic risk factors before we can assess the impact of contextual and situational changes on a defendant's immediate level of risk. Knowledge of these predictors is especially important for those dealing with sex offenders residing in the community: a relatively low-risk offender can suddenly become high risk for reoffending.

SEX OFFENDER TREATMENT

Because of the anger and fear generated by sex crimes, it is not uncommon for the public to view sex offender treatment with skepticism and resentment; they perceive it to be ineffective and an example of "coddling" criminals when retributive punishment seems more appropriate. Contemporary sex offender treatment, however, can play an important role in reducing sex offender recidivism and is almost always used in addition to a prison or probation sentence, not as a substitute for criminal justice intervention. In this section I shall explore several important questions surrounding sex offender treatment: What is involved in treating sex offenders? How has sex offender treatment changed over the years? How does it reduce recidivism? When does it work?

Several states offer prison-based treatment for sex offenders, and a growing trend is to mandate specialized treatment as part of a community-based sanction on probation or parole. Treatment, therefore, can occur in a multitude of settings and outcome studies regarding the effect of treatment on subsequent criminal behavior are impacted by the type of population under investigation (for example, institutional versus community-based). Contemporary sex offender therapy generally takes the form of cognitive-behavioral modification, with a focus on relapse prevention and victim-empathy, with the possibility of pharmacological augmentation. Surgical castration (biological therapy) is controversial on ethical and clinical grounds and is only occasionally used.

Although behavioral modification therapies are now the clinician intervention of choice, sex offender treatment modalities and perspectives have shifted through the years. Beginning in the 1930s (and lasting through the 1950s) society attempted to "cure" sick sex offenders using the medical model, which believed that sex offending behavior resulted from a devastating illness or disease. Today, the language and goals of sex offender therapy have changed to focus on management and control of sex offending behavior (Terry 2006). In the last seventy years, there have been three widespread approaches to treating sex offenders: psychotherapy, behavioral therapy, and psychopharmacological interventions (Barnes et al. 1994). Psychotherapy from the 1930s to the 1950s was the first specialized sex offender treatment; it required significant introspection on the part of offenders to enable them to understand their triggers and motivations for engaging in acts of sexual violence (Baker 1984). Psychotherapy techniques for sex offenders typically included individual and group therapy, family counseling (usually reserved for incest offenders),[5] victim-empathy lessons, acceptance of personal responsibility for offending, sex education classes, and cognitive restructuring (Barnes et al. 1994). Outcome studies did not support continual use of this treatment approach for serious sex offenders, especially when it was used as the only clinician intervention (Becker and Hunter 1992; Baker 1984).

Behavioral modification techniques became to appear in the 1950s and 1960s, primarily as a result of the lack of efficacy with traditional psychotherapeutic approaches (Marshall, Anderson, and Fernandez 1999). At this time, experts believed that sex crimes were the direct result of an offender's interest in criminal sexual stimuli. Therefore, the clinical approach to sex offenders involved the use of learning theory to teach sex offenders how to extinguish deviant behavior and replace it with socially acceptable interactions and responses. Some of the most commonly used behavioral treatment systems used to replace deviant sexual fantasies with socially acceptable ones were prosocial skills classes, assertiveness training, anger management, role-playing, aversive conditioning (McGuire and Vallance 1964), operant conditioning (Skinner 1953), covert sensitization, orgasmic reconditioning (Marques, 1970), and cognitive restructuring (Sapp and Vaughn 1991). The deviant sexual arousal patterns targeted for transformation included sexual violence against women, sexual interest in children, and homosexuality (Terry 2006).

By the 1970s, prominent sex offender researchers Gene Abel, William Marshall, and colleagues noted that existing behavioral modification treatments were not addressing many of the needs and issues prevalent among sex offending populations (Antonowicz and Valliant 1992; Barnes et al. 1994; Terry 2006). This recognition led to the creation of *cognitive-behavioral treatment,* a multimodal therapeutic approach designed to address the primary factors (socioeconomic, cognitive, behavioral, and emotional) believed to be at the root of sexual violence. Within the next ten years, cognitive-behavioral modification sex offender treatments were expanded to include relapse prevention techniques—currently considered a milestone in successful completion of sex offender therapy. Relapse prevention is so signal because it is believed to teach offenders how to "manage" their "incurable" criminal behavior (Marshall 1996). Several other notable additions to cognitive-behavioral modification therapies for sex offenders remain in use today. These additions include cognitive restructuring, victim-empathy, and the inclusion of objective testing mechanisms like the phallometric test (which measures penile arousal to visual and/or audio stimuli) and the polygraph examination. When deemed necessary, contemporary sex offender treatment can be augmented with psychotropic medications and/or hormonal therapies. Examples of some commonly used medical/hormonal treatments to reduce testosterone and sex drive are antiandrogen, antigonadotropin, and "chemical castration" (Depo-Provera) (Terry 2006, 153). Medical treatments are viewed as a means to help serious sex offenders, such as pedophiles, reduce their sexual interest and impulsive sexual behaviors.

If cognitive-behavioral modification treatments are well designed and implemented, they enable offenders to be fully aware of their sex crimes and accept personal responsibility for them, to understand the feelings and moods that led to their criminal behavior (the "red flags"), to restructure the distorted thinking that allowed them to justify their crimes (for example, believing that a young child was "flirting" with the offender), to take on positive and healthy attitudes and behaviors about sex and sexuality, to develop prosocial and appropriate skills, to identify their own sex offending triggers and high-risk situations, to comprehend the harm that their crimes caused to others, to know their own sexual offending cycle, and to develop a relapse prevention plan (Barnes et al. 1994; Lane Council of Governments 2003; Terry 2006).[6] According to this clinical approach, sexual criminality is a learned response that was reinforced by a positive outcome (or lack of negative consequences) during the offender's first sex crime (Terry 2006). The clinical approach, along with the tenets of deterrence and rational choice theories, suggests that "costs" (formal and informal) must be immediate and higher than the perceived benefits for engaging in deviant sexual behavior. Otherwise, deviant sexual arousal patterns (and subsequent sexually criminal behavior) may be reinforced and rewarded.

The issue of whether sex offender treatment "works" is still debated in academic and clinical circles. In large part, the controversy and contradictory findings (much as with recidivism research) are attributed to research-oriented problems. For instance, the impact that treatment has on future offending may vary based upon the sample being studied. Treatment populations made up of more serious sex offenders or of sex offenders who do not "buy into" the treatment mentality may be more likely to recidivate after treatment than sex offenders who do not have serious criminal or sex offense records and who agree to get help. Further, treatment groups composed of heterogeneous sex offender populations (with differing recidivism rates, sexual fixations and predispositions, and psychopathological conditions) may respond differently to therapeutic intervention. Unfortunately, we cannot determine likely success among homogenous categories of sex offenders (rapists, child molesters, pedophiles, exhibitionists, and so forth) because the treatment efficacy research on disaggregated samples is too sparse (Lane Council of Governments 2003).

Another methodological roadblock in assessing treatment efficacy is the lack of adequate comparisons or control groups. The design solution to this obstacle is to assign sex offenders (with similar attributes) randomly to either of two groups: one group receives treatment; the other (the control group) does not. Ethical considerations, however, forbid preventing willing recipients from receiving treatment services. No one wants to be the person who refused sex offender treatment to a willing subject— and who subsequently reoffends.

Variability in how treatment programs/researchers define and measure success is problematic for generalizing about the ability of sex offender treatment to deter future acts of sexual violence. Measurement devices consist of self-reports and computerized criminal justice data on arrest or conviction. As previously mentioned, these sources suffer from all the measurement error (and underreporting) problems addressed in the recidivism section; as such, their accuracy is questionable. Attrition is a further complication in assessing the efficacy of sex offender treatment. Treatment refusal and dropout rates are high among this population for a myriad of reasons, such as lack of motivation, financial constraints, and rearrest. Yet there is only limited agreement on how to handle the issue in terms of treatment outcome, resulting in additional inconsistency across studies.

Another hurdle in conducting global analysis on outcome studies is that treatment models often become quickly outdated (Marshall and Pithers 1994). This rapid obsolescence holds especially true for treatment geared toward reduction of sexual violence. The treatment protocol for sex offenders today is a vastly different landscape from that of only ten years ago. We cannot generalize with a high degree of certainty about the efficacy of any particular therapeutic intervention precisely because of its rapidly evolving nature.

Nevertheless, there are some consistent findings in studies evaluating cognitive-behavioral modification treatment models—which has been the preferred therapeutic intervention for the past decade—for sex offenders. Some recent meta-analysis work (analyzing the results of a large group of different studies) concludes that individuals who successfully completed treatment had lower official recidivism rates (for sex and nonsex crimes) than offenders who did not complete treatment. For example, a meta-analysis investigation that studied the treatment impact on approximately eleven thousand sex offenders (from seventy-nine different studies) determined that relapse prevention–based treatment reduced sexual rearrest by 10.4 percent (Alexander 1999). Similarly, another meta-analysis report encompassing forty-three studies and a combined total of over nine thousand sex offenders found that treated sexual criminals recidivated less often than untreated comparison/control groups: a 10 percent sexual recidivism rate for treated sex offenders compared to a 17 percent sexual recidivism rate for untreated offenders. Furthermore, sex offender treatment appears to reduce all criminal tendencies among sex offenders as the general (nonsexual) recidivism rate was also lower among treated sex offenders: 32 percent general recidivism rate for treated offenders compared to a 51 percent general recidivism rate for the comparison group members (Hanson 2000a). Stated simply, results across numerous studies indicate that treatment has a positive impact on sexual and nonsexual re-cidivism (Hanson 2000a; Salter 2003).

Even though sex offenders who complete treatment generally have lower official reoffense rates than their treatment failure counterparts, a "decay process" (loss of benefit) is often evident, albeit at different rates, for all groups of offenders (Hanson, Steffy, and Gautier 1993; Prentky, Lee, Knight, and Cerce 1997). Stated simply, the benefits of treatment dis-sipate with time. Research in the last twenty years has continually found that although child molesters who complete treatment often have lower recidivism rates than convicted child molesters who do not complete treat-ment, this population experiences slow and constant decay of therapeu-tic intervention and remains at risk to reoffend throughout their lifetime (Hanson, Steffy, and Gautier 1993; Prentky, Lee, Knight, and Cerce 1997). In other words, treatment is not a "quick and easy" fix to sexual violence nor should it be a stand-alone measure to control sex offenders. The pol-icy implications for these treatment findings appear straightforward: give priority to cognitive-behavioral modification treatment modalities and provide sufficiently long criminal justice interventions to reduce the risk of reoffense, thus offsetting the decay process. Long-term community supervision is warranted for high-risk offenders.

Incarceration, with or without treatment, and mandatory minimum sen-tences are today's preferred method for dealing with sex offenders. This approach may feed the criminal justice system's and the public's need to be "tough on crime," but it will inevitably result in many, if not most, sex offenders' being released back onto the streets, sans treatment or com-munity oversight because they are ineligible for probation or conventional parole. Unless criminal justice protocol considers empirical data in its philosophies and policies regarding how best to handle sex offenders, ju-dicial responses are unlikely to create significant inroads toward eradicat-ing sexual violence. I have demonstrated here that sex offender recidivism is far more complex than media representations and political rhetoric would lead one to assume. In the next chapter, I shall address what sets sex crimes apart from other violent offenses, explain the three significant waves of sex offender legislation (dating back from the 1930s to the present), and discuss the strengths and weaknesses of popular sex offen-der laws like community notification, involuntary civil commitment, and AMBER alerts.

Legal Warfare: Sex Offender Legislation

If you ask the average citizen to describe a sex offender you will probably get a picture of a drooling violent predator, either retarded or scheming, who rapes and kills women and children for sexual pleasure. If you ask what can be done about these offenders, responses will likely range from castration to electrocution because it is believed nothing less will stop them from offending again in the future. Such stereotypes do not reflect reality but they do drive criminal justice policy. Sex offenders have become the new bogeymen, used by politicians to intimidate and scare citizens concerned about public safety. Often the claims have more to do with scoring political points than creating a safer society.

—Eric Lotke, National Center on Institutions and Alternatives

In this chapter I investigate the ebb and flow of sex offender legislation over the last seventy-five years. I begin by establishing the way in which sex offenders are different from other violent criminals and why sex offenders are therefore responded to by lawmakers, the media, and the public in so unique a fashion. The three distinct periods of sex offender legislation will be covered along with an in-depth analysis on contemporary sex offender laws: sex offender registration, community notification, AMBER alerts, and the involuntary civil commitment of sex offenders. Additionally, I focus attention on what is known (and not known) about the ultimate implications of sex offender laws. Do they make communities safer or do they merely provide illusions of safety? Are they legitimate attempts at dealing with the problems associated with sexual violence or nothing more than rhetoric and oversimplified responses to complex social problems? Are they based on research findings or cloaked in half-truths and rumors as some experts suggest. Social policy can have positive or negative consequences; a comprehensive review of whether sex offender laws have made communities more or less safe is mandated.

WHY ARE SEX CRIMES DIFFERENT?

Public opinion surveys routinely show that citizens view crime as a serious social ill and believe that more punitive penalties are needed. The enhanced media attention received by some sex offenses (see chapter 1) has added to the overall level of panic about crime. Policymakers and legislatures have responded to the public's fear concerning sex offenders by treating them as a special category and creating both civil and criminal procedures to deal with sex crimes. In addition to the general concerns they raise about crime and violence, sex crimes are distinguished from other offenses by several factors.

First, sex offenses are different from many other serious crimes in that they have distinctive gendered offending and victimization characteristics. Known sex offenders are nearly always male (about 85 to 90 percent) and victims overwhelmingly female (85 to 90 percent) (Bureau of Justice Statistics 2004). This victimization pattern is atypical for many acts of violence. Males are overrepresented as victims of robbery, total assault, simple assault, and aggravated assault (Bureau of Justice Statistics 2004). Many social scientists rely heavily on feminist theory for an answer to this gendered crime type. This perspective views sexual violence, most especially rape, as an extension and exaggeration of patriarchal societies that favor male dominance and female submissiveness to men. Patriarchy can be thought of as a two-part system: structural and ideological (Dobash and Dobash 1979). The structural component ensures that men hold the positions of power and influence that guarantees their role as the superior sex. The ideology establishes the foundation for men's superiority to women to be perceived as predetermined, natural and God's intention (DeKeseredy and Schwartz 1998). In this climate, both sexes are taught that males have sexual entitlement over females. Additionally, it has been asserted that sexual violence rewards all men, even non–sex offenders, because it preserves men's dominance over women (Scully 1994). As further evidence of the socialized nature of sex crimes, negative attitudes about women and men's adherence to rape myths are among the most consistent predictors of male-on-female perpetrated violence (Belknap 2001; Scully 1994).

The violent impact that patriarchal beliefs have upon women is most pronounced among those populations of men where associations with male peers are especially influential—such as all-male sports teams and fraternities. Men who believe they are entitled to disrespect women (and surround themselves by other males who condone this behavior) are more likely to engage in sexual, physical, and emotional abuse against women (DeKeseredy and Schwartz 1998). The concentration of male sports activities and fraternities (and the alcohol consumption that often accompanies coed social functions) on college campuses is likely a contributing factor to the increased risk of sexual assault among college women, compared to similar age groups of women who do not attend college (Fisher, Cullen, and Turner 2000).

Finally, as indicated in chapter 1 victims of sexual assault suffer from a host of unique short- and long-term physical and emotional consequences. Psychological fallout ranges from Rape Trauma Syndrome, psychosomatic disorders, anxiety, depression, and substance abuse; the latter is often used as a form of self-medication to numb the emotional pain associated with sexual victimization. The psychological trauma of being sexually assaulted by someone known to the victim is even more devastating than the emotional distress associated with other forms of victimization where the offender and victim know each other (Conte and Schuerman 1987). Although most sex crimes do not involve the use of a weapon (Bureau of Justice Statistics 2004) some victims have been killed in the course of their attack while others have been forced to contend with physical injuries, sexually transmitted diseases (Meadows 2001), and chronic pain disorders (Koss and Heslet 1992).

These factors, in combination with the heightened public concern and fear following numerous highly publicized vicious attacks on children by convicted sex offenders, have culminated in an aggressive social policy campaign to fight sexual violence. In addition to such criminal sanctions as mandatory prison terms (for example, the twenty-five-year prison sentence that the Florida legislature just passed for offenders convicted of sexually assaulting victims under the age of twelve) and lifetime community supervision, sex offender laws now constitute a host of civil laws and policies. Criminal laws are designed with the explicit goal of achieving retribution and deterrence of sex offenders. The role of deterrence on sexual violence was specifically addressed in the introductory chapter and as such will not be further debated here.

Nevertheless, courts and legislators have waged an equally aggressive attack against sex offenders in the civil courts. On this legal stage, sex offender registration, community notification, AMBER alerts, and civil commitment statutes presumably have different objectives than they would in the criminal courts. For instance, in the civil legal arena, concepts such as "regulation" and "community safety" replace the terminology of punishment and deterrence that are part of the current criminal justice philosophy. Whether sex offender laws are protective in nature or in fact constitute additional punishment remains a hotly contested issue in the judicial community, although the legal battle on the issue appears to be final (*Kansas v Hendricks* 1997).[1]

THE HISTORICAL DEVELOPMENT OF SEX OFFENDER LAWS

Sociolegal scholars have identified three distinctive periods of sex offender laws. The first wave of sex offender statutes started in the 1930s when legislatures began passing "sexual psychopath" laws as a response to several violent and sexually charged attacks against children and young adults. In 1937, J. Edgar Hoover, as head of the Federal Bureau of Investigation (FBI), declared a "war on sex crimes" and demanded that citizens and authorities do everything possible to curtail—what he believed to be—the ever-growing problem of sexual violence (Lucken and Latina 2002). Although official documents indicated that sex crimes were on the rise, a close examination of the records indicates that most of the arrests were for homosexual activities between consenting adults. This finding caused legal historians to question whether this wave of sex offender legislation was motivated, at least partially, by homophobia (Freedman 1987).

During this time period the *New York Times* was routinely printing more than thirty-five articles a week highlighting sexual violence, a favorite theme being stories that focused on bizarre murder–sexual assaults of children (Lucken and Latina 2002). In the mid-1930s, Albert Fish's crimes offered an exemplar. He sexually molested and then brutally killed and cannibalized a twelve-year old boy. Apparently, Fish's heinousness extended beyond this crime; he was believed to have sexually victimized and mutilated countless other children (Terry 2006). These extremely unusual events captivated the media and resulted in widespread fear and panic over sex offenders and their deeds.

The sexual psychopath laws passed during the 1930s attempted to cure "sick" sex offenders and divert them out of the prison system via the mental health arena, where the emphasis was treatment and preventive detention.

The emerging popularity of progressivism and a belief that rehabilitation could be achieved through state-sanctioned measures spurred the popularity of these laws. By the end of the 1950s, some twenty-six states and the District of Columbia had involuntary commitments for "sexual psychopaths."[2] Despite their national appeal, sexual psychopath laws were not standardized in terms of how they treated offenders or even in their diagnostic and release criteria. Over the next ten years the public began to lose faith in the rehabilitation of offenders. Eventually even the clinical community shied away from the idea of treatment and civil commitment of sex offenders and declared the term "sexual psychopath" meaningless.

The late 1960s, a period punctuated by radicalism and reform, mark the start of the second wave of sex offender policies (Lieb et al. 1998). The impetus of this sex offender legislation is distinct from both the first and third wave of sex offender laws because it did not follow a series of child rape and murders. Rather, the second wave of sex offender laws was a result of social movements (civil rights, offender's rights, and women's rights) and changes in what the public believed the goals of punishment should be. The role of government in preventing and deterring violence was questioned by the public as was the nature and fairness by which "outlaws" and "deviants" were identified and labeled (Lucken and Latina 2002). Concerns were raised that the sexual psychopath laws of the previous era were ineffective, ambiguous, and too subjective in their admission and release criteria—all of which presented civil liberty complications for offenders detained under these laws. These concerns, along with a "nothing works" mentality, resulted in a dramatic repeal of the sexual psychopath laws. Individuals previously confined in state mental hospitals were now sent to prison instead (Dorsett 1998).

By the 1970s efforts were in full force to refocus attention to the wider problem of violence against women and children (Finkelhor 1984; Pleck 1987). Women's groups, often through grassroots efforts, raised awareness of the magnitude and pervasiveness of sexual violence in intimate relationships and family settings and challenged the image that rapists were all crazed beasts that lurked in dark alleys. Feminists asserted that the recognition was essential to refiguring sexual violence as a widespread cultural problem (Wells and Motley 2001). Victims' advocates pushed for legislative changes on a national scale that would (1) encourage victims to report their assaults to authorities; (2) enhance the support and responsiveness of the law enforcement community to issues of violence against women; and (3) help protect the interests and privacy of assault victims

(Spohn and Horney 1992). Although symbolic success was achieved when these measures were implemented, real improvement for victims of most types of sex crimes (assaults by nonstrangers) remains elusive.[3]

Advocates and researchers worked in tandem to achieve the goal of convincing legislators that male-on-female–perpetrated violence was not merely an individual psychopathology, but a serous social problem requiring governmental action (Ford et al. 2002). In 1972, the Bureau of Justice Statistics started to track victimizations through the National Crime Victimization Survey, which included sexual assault information. In 1978, the U.S. Commission on Civil Rights and other federal committees consulted with researchers regarding the extent of battering and violence endured by women at the time. By the late 1980s, the federal government was committed to funding research on family and intimate partner violence that occurs in domestic settings. Rape reform legislation and congressional mandates such as the 1994 Violence Against Women Act (that was renewed in 2000 and is currently awaiting 2005 reauthorization) publicly acknowledge the seriousness of sexual assaults and crimes against women and children generally (Ford et al. 2002). According to the Department of Justice's July 2005 U.S. congressional report on the reauthorization of the Violence Against Women Act, VAWA's grant program has allocated more than one billion dollars to fund research and establish deterrence and victim assistance programs in the areas of battering, stalking, child victimization, and sex crimes.

By the 1990s, the third and most recent wave of civil sex offender laws was unfolding (sex offender registration, community notification, AMBER alerts and preventive detention). Public attention on sexual violence was again catapulted into the national consciousness because of several highly publicized, sexually charged violent assaults against children by unknown assailants. Obviously, child victimization by strangers exerts a powerful influence over the public and lawmakers despite these crimes' being statistically uncommon. Scholars argue that historically our responses to these types of sex crimes constitute a moral panic over the possibility that strangers will sexually molest and murder our children (Jenkins 1998).[4] Moral panic may ensue after one of these crimes because "citizens cannot understand a sex attack on a child, and this incomprehensibility fuels reactions of fear. . . . The attack and investigation become front-page news . . . describing the failure of the justice system to protect vulnerable persons, which fuels a strong public reaction. . . . Government officials then feel compelled to act" (Lieb et al. 1998, 11).

Because the third wave of sex offender legislation was prompted by attacks committed against children by unknown or barely known assailants, this statistically small scenario becomes the primary focus of the laws. This disproportionate response explains why registration and community notification do not target offenders who are most at risk for committing acts of sexual violence (family members and acquaintances), but concentrate instead on stranger-danger types of offenses. Unfortunately, this skewed focus also means that contemporary sex offender legislation is unlikely to stop sex offenders or end the larger problem of sexual violence. The following section focuses on the laws directed at sex offenders.

SEX OFFENDER REGISTRATION AND COMMUNITY NOTIFICATION

Sex offender registration laws, designed to assist law enforcement in the investigation of sex crimes, have been in existence for decades.[5] Community notification mandates are relatively new and are designed to empower citizens by providing them with information about convicted sex offenders in their area. The first community notification legislation was enacted in Washington State in 1990 after the sexual assault and mutilation of a young Tacoma boy by a paroled sex offender, Earl Shriner—who had warned authorities of his continuing fantasies to rape and mutilate children prior to his release from prison. On July 2, 1994, a seven-year-old Hamilton, New Jersey, girl named Megan Kanka was raped and asphyxiated by her thirty-three-year-old neighbor, Jesse Timmendequas. Mr. Timmendequas was a convicted child molester who, along with two other paroled sex offenders, resided near the Kanka family. The brutal nature of this rape and murder hurled the issue of sexual violence against children into the national spotlight (Avrahamian 1998). As noted in chapter 1, these brutal attacks against innocent children led to the swift enactment of mandatory registration and community notification, commonly referred to as "Megan's Law." This package of sex offender statutes was proposed to protect the community, specifically children, by requiring convicted sex offenders to register with their local law enforcement agencies upon conviction or release. Differences exist in sex offender registration and community notification laws because there are no national standards to guide the application of the community notification process.

Universally, the most sensitive and controversial aspect of the law is community notification, whereby information about the offender's name and residence is available to the public. It is becoming increasingly common for an offender's picture, work address, and residence to be available on the Internet. In some states, highway billboard signs post the sex offender's name, address, and photo under a caption reading something like "Beware: Sex Offender Lives Near You" (Moreno 1997). In other locales, residents can receive a notification in the mail with the sex offender's name and picture listed. In other jurisdictions, such as Delaware, the defendant's driver's license contains a special mark designating him/her as a sexual offender. The invasive labeling of sex offenders is necessary, according to Mrs. Kanka: "If I had known that three sex perverts were living across the street from me, Megan would be alive today" (Steinbock 1995, 7).

Mrs. Kanka is not alone in her belief that a sex offender's information should be accessible to the public. The support for this legislation is demonstrated not only by the swift passage of Megan's Law itself (which the state of New Jersey adopted only weeks after Megan's murder), but also by the fact that within the same year, sixteen other state legislatures had written similar policies. In 1996, the U.S. Congress passed legislation (Jacob Wetterling Act followed by the Pam Lyncher Act) that required all states to provide some form of community notification of convicted sex offenders (Finn 1997).[6]

In 1997, then Attorney General Janet Reno stated that federal registration and notification legislation was necessary because "the Bureau of Justice Statistics report shows that accurate registries and effective community notification programs are at the heart of our fight against sex offenders" (U.S. Department of Justice, 1997, *supra* n. 31). The contention, however, that sex offender registries are the "heart" of the battle against sexual violence is questionable. For instance, the very report Attorney General Reno cites demonstrates statistical evidence that most sex offenders are *known assailants*, not the strangers that are the focus of registries (Greenfeld 1997). By the next year, all fifty states had sex offender registration and community notification laws. State statutes vary regarding which types of offenders are subject to community notification, the intensity of the notification process, and the sensitivity of offender information made available to the public. Some states require broad dissemination of information about certain tiers of sex offenders to local organizations, community residents, and media (New Jersey, Oregon, and Washington take this approach). A second group of states gives probation and parole officers discretion to notify anyone they choose with information about released sex offenders (Connecticut, Georgia, and New York engage in this practice). A third group authorizes public disclosure of sex offender information for any purpose to any person who submits a written request to the county sheriff or local police. The information provided may be about a named individual or about all registrants in a geographical area (Alaska, Michigan, South Carolina, Vermont, and Virginia follow this directive).

Although the passage and enactment of community notification legislation has transpired rather uneventfully, the laws themselves have encountered constitutional challenges. The legal challenges associated with sex offender registration and community notification laws have come in many forms. For instance, Fifth Amendment (double jeopardy) concerns surround the issue of whether sex offenders are punished more than once for the same crime when they are required to register and are subjected to community notification, in addition to the sanctions imposed on them at the time of sentencing. Ex post facto constitutional protections are in place to make sure that offenders are not punished by laws that were not in effect at the time the crime was committed. The concern arises for legal scholars because sex offender registration and community notification requirements are often retroactive in their application—meaning they apply to offenders who were convicted of sex crimes prior to the existence of these laws. Due process issues pertaining to sex offender registration and community notification and protections against cruel and unusual (that is, excessive) punishment have also brought challenges against these laws. Initially, these claims were met with mixed success in the courts (DeMatteo 1998). For instance, the federal courts in New Jersey, Louisiana, Connecticut, and Oregon have ruled both for and against the retroactive application of the law. Despite vigorous attacks by civil libertarians, community notification laws have suffered only minor legal setbacks. Several State Supreme Courts, U.S. Circuit Courts, and now the U.S. Supreme Court have upheld the laws and ruled in favor of sex offender registration and community notification.

In 2003, the U.S. Supreme Court determined it was constitutional for states to post photographs of convicted sex offenders on the Internet (*Connecticut Department of Public Safety v John Doe*). Relying on 1976 precedent in the *Paul v Davis* right to privacy case—where the Court found that convicted persons could have their court records made public so long as it did not infringe on their freedom—it was determined that the posting of sex offender photographs on the Internet did not violate an offender's due process protections because damaging one's reputation did not amount to an impediment to their freedom. In a separate case, the

U.S. Supreme Court rejected the argument that mandatory registration violated ex post facto protections and demanded that sex offenders comply with registration and notification guidelines in their state, regardless of whether they were in effect at the time of the offender's sex offense conviction (*Otte v Doe*).

Are We Now Protected from Sex Offenders?

Sex offender registration requires convicted sex offenders to notify law enforcement of their residential status (and any changes) for a specified period of time. Community notification laws make this information available to the public. Not much is understood about the sociological implications or effectiveness of sex offender registration and community notification. A 1988 California study on sex offender registration and recidivism of convicted sex offenders found that mandated registration was effective in helping identify, locate, and arrest suspected sex offenders. The law's impact on sexual recidivism, however, was insignificant; the rate of recidivism among sex offenders and non–sex offenders was not statistically different (Lewis 1988). In 1995, a study was conducted (in Washington State) on the impact of community notification on sexual reoffending. Once again, researchers found the law produced no statistically significant difference in rearrest rates. Sex offenders subjected to community notification were just as likely to be arrested for new sex crimes as they had been before the law was implemented (Schram and Milloy 1995).

There are logistical complications with registration and notification. Collection, maintenance, enforcement, and the notification process are expensive and labor-intensive (Zevitz and Farkas 2000). Also, lists are likely to be incomplete and inaccurate as offenders change residences frequently or refuse to cooperate—a common problem known as displacement (Terry 2006). Because of the stigma associated with community notification, offenders often move to other communities and may not notify officials of the change. An investigation conducted in Tennessee revealed that 28 percent of convicted sex offenders moved from their registered communities and then failed to reregister (Finn 1997). Other studies found that registration compliance of convicted sex offenders with law enforcement authorities fared no better than 25 to 54 percent nationally (Avrahamian 1998).

A potential unintended consequence of registration and notification mandates are that individuals convicted of consensual acts of sodomy are required to register as sex offenders. In this regard, some contend that community notification statutes reinforce antigay sentiment by mandating registration for sodomy convictions and encouraging police officers to use undercover tactics to apprehend gays (Small 1999). Homophobia's role in sex crime prosecution was an issue with several of the interview respondents who were part of this research. A handful of male sex offenders (those reporting themselves to be gay or bisexual) who agreed to be interviewed said that they were arrested and placed on probation after an Internet sting operation targeting "male only" chat rooms uncovered sexual conversations between themselves and others who self-identified as boys under the age of eighteen. In actuality, the offenders were corresponding with undercover police officers posing as minors.

Despite the widespread belief to the contrary, there is no evidence to suggest that there is any link between homosexuality and criminal sex offending behavior (Pratt 1998). Given the lack of danger posed by gays and lesbians—and the rarity of stranger-danger—it certainly seems that there are more productive and victim-oriented ways to allocate scarce criminal justice resources. For instance, education platforms targeted to parents and citizens about the typical sex offender profile and victim-offender relationships or increased funding for sex offender treatment programs in prison could be more productive programs. The efficacy of community notification is only compromised by including persons who pose no safety risk to the community on sex offender registries.

We must hope that the practice of registering individuals convicted of consensual acts of sodomy as sex offenders will stop. In June 2003 (*Lawrence v Texas*), the U.S. Supreme Court ruled all sodomy laws illegal, citing a constitutional right to sexual privacy. This landmark decision reversed a 1986 ruling (*Bowers v Hardwick*) that restricted some forms of consensual sexual contact between couples even in the privacy of their own homes. It is too soon to predict what the ripple effect of the *Lawrence* decision will have in terms of gay rights in general; at the very least, the thirteen states that still have sodomy laws will no longer be able to selectively prosecute private, consensual homosexual acts and require that these names be on sex offender registration lists.[7] The more accurately registries list dangerous and predatory sex offenders, the more likely they are to identify those who genuinely pose a risk to women and children.

There are historical incidents of antigay sentiments in sex offender legislation as well. One of the factors behind the first wave of sex offender legislation was an alleged association between psychosis and criminality. This purported relationship between psychopathology and crime, coupled with the notion at the time that homosexuality was "caused" by mental illness, resulted in widespread support for sex offender laws in the 1930s (Pratt 1998). Widespread support for sexual psychopath laws also resulted from the misplaced fear that same-sex conduct was synonymous with pedophilia (Pratt 1998) and that gay men actively "recruited" children for sex. According to one author, the initial wave of sex offender legislation was so saturated with homophobia that it was questionable whether the term "sexual psychopath" was merely another way to say homosexual (Freedman 1987). It was not until the government surrendered its goal of forging a single definition of sexual morality (and instead prioritized community safety) that sexual psychopath laws were revised, no longer targeting adult consensual same sex relations (La Fond 1999).

There are other problems with community notification laws. For example, while notification laws are criticized for being overinclusive, they are concomitantly riddled with problems of being underinclusive in that many offenders are able to avoid registration through plea negotiations. For example, it is common for offenders to enter plea negotiations for offenses that do not carry the registration mandate. A "successful" plea agreement does not negate an offender's potential risk. Many of the non-mandated registrants may be equally dangerous, if not more dangerous, than registered offenders (Avrahamian 1998; Freeman-Longo 1996). For example, Richard Allen Davis, the individual convicted in California of the highly publicized sexual assault and murder of Polly Klaas, had previously served fifteen years in prison for sex crimes, dating back to 1973. Because of plea negotiations, however, he was able to avoid convictions for the specific sex offenses that would have required him to register (Steinbock 1995). And Leroy Hendricks, the defendant who fought the constitutionality of sexually dangerous persons' civil commitment statutes was himself released from custody many times after accepting plea negotiations for reduced sentences. Furthermore, it must be acknowledged that because sex crimes are severely underreported and few offenders are ever caught, registration legislation applies to only the small percentage of offenders who are identified, apprehended and convicted of committing certain sex crimes (Avrahamian 1998; DeMatteo 1998; Friedland 1999; Small 1999).

Because sex offender registration and community notification target the "stranger" sexual assailant and make no provisions to protect children who fall prey to sexual offenses at the hands of a known assailant, sex offender laws perpetuate an inaccurate image of harm. Estimates indicate that 85 percent of all child sexual abuse (and more than 95 percent of the abuse against children under the age of six) is committed by family members and friends (Snyder 2000). Sexual victimization data collected on persons twelve years of age and older indicate a similar pattern (Bureau of Justice Statistics 2004). Consequently, sex offender registration laws imbue a false sense of security by leading communities into believing they can protect children from sex offenders by keeping them away from the men on these lists. As stated elsewhere, most child molesters are not crazed, savage, beastlike strangers. Rather, many sex offenders hold positions of authority and trust and are relatives, friends, neighbors, or acquaintances of the child. The same holds true for most of the men included in this analysis. More than 50 percent of the male sex offenders discussed in the following pages have high school diplomas or college degrees and eight out of ten assaulted a relative or someone they already knew. To reiterate: sex offender registration and community notification legislation fails to target the offenders who pose the greatest risk to children (relatives and friends). Therefore, at most it can hope to identify only about 15 percent of unknown offenders. Thus this type of legislation is unlikely to be efficacious at curbing sexual violence in any measurable way.

Not only is there no empirical evidence that sex offender laws provide for safer communities, questions also remain regarding the overall effect the labeling and public branding of an individual as "sex offender" is likely to have. Because many states now make their sex offender registries accessible to the public on the Internet (and the U.S. Supreme Court has approved the practice), the availability of this information has grown from the confines of a local community to being but a computer stroke away to the entire world. This change in accessibility is likely to increase the degree of public stigmatization felt by offenders. The notification process may further alienate the offender, increasing feelings of detachment and anger and making it more difficult for registered offenders to find housing and employment—thereby enhancing their likelihood of reoffending (Avrahamian 1998; Braithwaite 1989; Hall and Proctor 1987; Hanson, Scott, and Steffy 1995; Zevitz and Farkas 2000). "Because low-level offenders pose minimal risk of reoffense, the harms of loss of reputation and anonymity along with the stigma of being branded a sex offender could outweigh the protective value of public notification" (Small 1999). Therefore, responsible public policy calls for courts and policymakers to consider the potential harms caused by these laws (including loss of employment, residential stability, loss of support networks) against the potential risks or dangerousness a particular offender poses to the community (Zevitz and Farkas 2000). Community shaming and stigmatization, without concern for therapeutic reintegration, will likely increase the risks of recidivism. A "one size fits all" sex offender registration and notification is not in the best interest of social justice or community safety.

There is also an increased risk of attack by vigilantes. In the context of sex crimes, vigilantism comes in either the form of ostracism or acts of individual violence and retribution (Small 1999). For instance, according to one report, 26 percent of registered sex offenders are the target of some public harassment (Bedarf 1998); the finding was replicated in this research. Specifically, 40 percent of the men on sex offender probation who were interviewed talked openly about their fears and experiences with vigilante justice. Public stigmatization, social isolation, and vigilantism are increased when names and addresses of sex offenders are released into the community. "We're turning [the offender] into a pariah, and creating situations where he is more likely to re-offend," reports Nadine Strossen, president of the American Civil Liberties Union. "Megan's Law is more about politics than it is about public safety."[8] Incidents of vigilante attacks have been reported in Washington, New Jersey, and other locales around the country (Small 1999). At times, these acts of vigilante justice are extreme. For example, in the state of Washington, hours before the highly publicized release of a sex offender, his house was burned to the ground (Avrahamian 1998). In the state of New Jersey a released sex offender had his home riddled with bullets after a bulletin was released notifying community members of his presence (Small 1999). "Released sex offenders may find it extremely difficult to re-assimilate into society. Problems finding and maintaining employment, securing housing, and making and keeping social relationships are the inevitable results of the stigma attached to the label 'sex offender'" (Small 1999). As we shall see in forthcoming chapters, the men in this study worried about vigilante justice being imposed on them while they were on probation. In *Doe v Poritz* (1995) the U.S. Supreme Court stated that they had faith in the public and media's ability to handle sex offender registration information responsibly and nonpunitively.

AMBER ALERTS

Another type of legislation inspired by the tragedy of a child victimized by a stranger is the AMBER Alert System (America's Missing: Broadcast Emergency Response). The program is designed to disseminate news rapidly regarding kidnapped children by publicizing the information over the radio and television and by posting electronic highway signs. The system itself was first created in 1996 after a nine-year old girl, Amber Hagerman, was abducted outside her Arlington, Texas, neighborhood while riding her bicycle on a sunny Saturday afternoon. Neighbors reported hearing Amber scream and witnessed a man drag Amber off her bike and pull her into his truck before speeding away. The kidnapping riveted the local community and generated a tremendous amount of media attention. Four days after her disappearance, Amber's body was recovered from a drainage ditch only a short distance from her home. Her throat had been slashed. Interviews with neighbors provided police and the FBI with a description of the suspect and his vehicle. Although authorities searched extensively for the killer, the crime was never solved. The community responded to this kidnapping and murder by forming a partnership between law enforcement officials and area broadcasters. The AMBER system was modeled after severe weather warning alert systems: it repeats news bulletins, over the radio, and across the television screen, about the abducted child and any details pertaining to the kidnapper's description and the type of vehicle used; help from viewers is requested.

A federal version of the program was signed into law by George W. Bush in May 2003. Given that all fifty states now participate in the AMBER system it is easier to extend AMBER alerts across state lines. In addition, federal funding has been allocated to states to help offset the costs associated with training law enforcement and media professionals on how to operate the system, when to enact an alert, and to purchase the necessary software and hardware to enact an actual alert.[9] Also included in the federal version of the law is an "add on" section of the bill that allows federal judges to levy more punitive sanctions when sentencing sex criminals.[10] For instance, judges can order sex offenders (only) to serve lifetime terms of probation (community supervision for life) once they are released from prison and mandatory life sentences can be imposed for two-time sex offenders of children.[11]

Effectiveness of the Policy

It is too early to accurately assess the efficacy of AMBER alerts. Anecdotal data, however, suggests that there have been some positive results, especially when the offender is known to the victim and victim's family. Newspaper accounts claim as many as sixty-eight children nationwide have been rescued as a direct result of AMBER alerts (*Seattle Times,* May

8, 2003). Further, since the AMBER alert system became federal law, more than 80 percent of the AMBER alert child abductions have resulted in successful recoveries (U.S. Department of Justice 2005).[12] Advocates proclaim that the recovery of these children results from increased public awareness, advances in technology, strong cooperation between law enforcement and the public, the media, and communities across state lines joining forces for the sake of the children. Timing of an alert is important, as 44 percent of stranger-abductions result in the child's murder within the first hour and 91 percent within twenty-four hours of the kidnapping (PBSJ 2004). Fortunately, most abductions do not occur at the hands of dangerous strangers.

An example of a recent AMBER alert success story occurred on May 7, 2005, in Taylorsville, Utah. A five-year old girl and her mother's drug-addicted fiancé went out to run errands. When they did not return as expected, the frantic mother called authorities, who then issued an AMBER alert on behalf of the missing child. Based on a radio broadcast of the disappearance and suspect's car, a citizen recognized the vehicle and notified police. The little girl was recovered without further incident. Yet another success story occurred on March 26, 2005, in Greenville, South Carolina. A father abducted his one-year old after allegedly assaulting the child's mother. As the suspect traveled on the highway, he became aware of the AMBER alert electronic signs detailing his vehicle and license plate number. The suspect contacted police and demanded the alert be cancelled. The authorities traced the suspect's cellular phone from this call and recovered the child a short time later.[13]

As these illustrations highlight, AMBER alerts have facilitated the recovery of children. Success stories like these provide optimism for parents and child advocates alike. It should be noted, however, that the successes associated with AMBER alerts appear strongly correlated with the victim-offender relationship. In other words, children who are abducted by a family member or friend appear more likely to be located and recovered safely than a child taken by an unknown assailant. This prognosis makes sense; obviously, the known offender's identity and vehicle information are readily available. Nonetheless, limitations to locating missing children remain. For instance, the families of underage runaways are excluded from AMBER alert recovery attempts. Experts claim that the prevalence of children running away from home makes it impossible for the AMBER alert system to be successful or taken seriously.[14] Child runaways are simply too common for the emergency alert system to be a feasible option.

Of course, even well-intentioned legislation may lead to complications and unanticipated consequences, and AMBER alerts are not likely to remain immune. Because the accuracy of the AMBER alerts often rests on eyewitness testimony (which is often faulty), misinformation regarding suspect and/or vehicle characteristics is likely to be transmitted over the airwaves. Also, there are already documented cases of full-blown AMBER alerts that resulted from false abduction reports being filed with police. False reports are dangerous in many regards. Crying wolf may engender apathy among the public so that they do not take the alerts seriously when they occur. The alerts could be used as a weapon between battling parents engaged in hostile child custody suits. They could also be used to divert suspicion from the real assailant.

For instance, the first AMBER alert enacted in the state of Maryland (February 2003) was from a call for help from a young father who reported that his two-month-old daughter had been abducted by the driver of an unlicensed cab. It turned out that the twenty-year-old father, Kenneth Jenkins, had murdered the infant and disposed of her body in a trash can. He was eventually charged with first-degree murder for killing the little girl. At one point in time, half of Maryland's AMBER alerts were based on what were later determined to be false abduction reports, leaving policymakers concerned that "the tool for finding missing children will come to be regarded as car alarms are—more often ignored than heeded" (*Baltimore Sun*, May 20, 2003). Finally, false abduction reports, and the ensuing alerts, result in the misuse and abuse of scarce law enforcement resources—potentially placing other victims at greater risk of harm, as police may not be able to respond to actual distress calls so expeditiously as they would be otherwise.

INVOLUNTARY CIVIL COMMITMENT

As of 2003, sex offender civil commitment statutes have been enacted in at least sixteen states, plus the District of Columbia, and proposed in more than thirty others. Contemporary sex offender laws are different from their predecessors. The wording is different (sexual psychopath laws are now called sexual predator laws),[15] the goals are different (punitive versus rehabilitative), and the sheer volume and type of sex offender laws have increased dramatically. The primary distinction to the contemporary sexual predator laws are the fact they are used to augment prison terms, rather than as an alternative to incarceration. The term *sexual predator* is now used with increasing frequency to describe repeat sex offenders. Prior to 1992, this term was virtually nonexistent in sociolegal literature. "The emergence of sex offenders as uncontrollable moral 'monsters' replaced earlier notions of sex offenders who were viewed as sick and diseased individuals in need of treatment" (La Fond 1999). Today's civil commitment laws allow states to detain a sex offender indefinitely under the pretense of preventive detention. Although there are variations from state to state, most existing sexual violent predator laws have the defendant transferred to a secure mental health facility, usually housed on prison grounds, once the state invokes the civil commitment process (Moreno 1997).[16] Typical commitment procedures require that the state demonstrate (1) prior sexually violent behavior of the defendant; (2) that the defendant suffers from a current mental abnormality or disorder; (3) that there is a likelihood of future violent sex acts; and (4) that the defendant's mental abnormality or disorder contributes to the likelihood of future dangerousness (Janus 1997).[17] The procedural due process requirements are that at a minimum, the state's findings be established at a "clear and convincing level"; in some instances the evidentiary requirement is elevated to proof beyond a reasonable doubt (Dorsett 1998).

Although these statutes rely on procedures that permit holding offenders *after* they have served their criminal sentences in full, the laws are able to sidestep issues of questionable constitutionality by calling the incapacitation "regulation" rather than "punishment." The U.S. Supreme Court (1987) previously ruled that the government's interest in "preventing danger to the community is a legitimate regulatory goal" and one that supersedes interests of individual liberty (*United States v Salerno*). In other words, according to the *Salerno* Court, if the primary intention of a statute is to protect the community from future harm (and not merely serve as a form of retribution or punishment), preventive detention is constitutional.

Background to Today's Civil Commitment Statute

On August 17, 1994, the state of Kansas sought civil commitment of Leroy Hendricks as a sexually violent predator; with this case, the constitutional battle regarding civil commitment of sex offenders began.[18] Mr. Hendricks had a sexually violent history dating back to 1955 when he pled guilty to indecent exposure. In 1956, he served a brief period of incarceration for another incident of "lewdness" against a female child. In 1960, he sexually assaulted two young boys and was sentenced to two years in prison. Seven years later, the state of Kansas convicted Hendricks for sexually molesting two more children (a male and female) for which he served another short incarceration. In 1984, Kansas again charged Hendricks for child molestation, this time against two thirteen-year-old boys. Although the defendant met the criteria outlined in the Habitual Criminal Act (three prior felony convictions), the state opted not to pursue Habitual Criminal charges, which could have tripled his sentence. Rather, the defendant pled guilty to two far less serious charges of indecent liberties with a minor and received the minimum sentence on each count. The judge sentenced Mr. Hendricks to five to twenty years in prison. Ten years into his sentence, Kansas filed a petition charging the defendant as a sexually violent predator. Hendricks attempted to have the petition dismissed on technical grounds. The court ruled against Hendricks and ordered him to undergo a psychological evaluation. The results of this evaluation indicated that Hendricks met the clinical diagnosis of pedophilia. Later, a trial was conducted and Hendricks was found "mentally abnormal" as defined in the Kansas Sexually Violent Persons statute.[19]

Hendricks filed suit alleging that Kansas's civil commitment statute was unconstitutional. Hendricks argued that the law violated his protection against double jeopardy, ex post facto, failed to ensure due process protection, and that the wording of the legislation was over broad and vague. The Kansas Supreme Court ruled in Hendricks's favor and found that the statute did, in fact, violate the Due Process Clause of the Fourteenth Amendment.[20] The legal battle, however, was not over. The state of Kansas petitioned the U.S. Supreme Court for certiorari. Hendricks then cross-petitioned the Court and reasserted his double jeopardy and ex post facto claims.

On June 23, 1997, in a five to four decision, the U.S. Supreme Court upheld the Kansas Sexually Violent Predator Act; in doing so, it ruled that the Kansas statute did satisfy substantive due process.[21] The Court found that an individual's freedom, though a central concern of due process, is not absolute in civil cases. Substantive requirements for civil commitment had only to meet a two-part standard: (1) a finding of "dangerousness" and (2) "some additional factor."[22] Thus, the Court ruled that a prerequisite of civil commitment required a factual finding of dangerousness to one's self or others and a finding of "mental illness" or "mental abnormality." The Court held that because Hendricks had a prior history of sexually molesting children, his risk of "dangerousness" was automatically established. The Court reasoned that having two distinct components or requirements of civil commitment served as a safeguard to limit involuntary civil confinement to those who suffer from a "volitional impairment rendering them dangerous beyond their control" (*Kansas v Hendricks* 1997, 14).

Issues and Public Safety Concerns

One of the loudest objections to involuntary civil commitment stems from its potential for abuse; indeed, many legal questions were left unanswered in the Hendricks ruling (Dorsett 1998; Moreno 1997). For instance, the Court did not address whether the statute may be extended to other groups of offenders or individuals who meet the criteria of suffering from an uncontrollable mental abnormality that puts the community at risk. One could argue that drug addicts and alcoholics suffer from mental and physical cravings for their drug of choice that are extreme enough to render them powerless to stop these urges. These individuals may be classified as dangerous persons if, say, the alcoholic had a previous DUI charge or the addict committed a theft to pay for her drugs. If a court were convinced (with the degree of evidentiary proof necessary) that these individuals are sufficiently high-risk to commit additional harmful acts, they could meet the criteria designated in the Kansas Sexually Violent Persons statute to be civilly committed.

The civil commitment process requires that a sex offender be identified as "dangerous." Deprivation of liberty based upon predictions of future dangerousness is ethically and clinically problematic. For instance, there are ethical concerns of incapacitating individuals based on actions they are *predicted* to commit in the future versus incapacitating them for actions they have *already* committed. It is possible that because civil detention is justified on projections of future violence rather than actual behavior, civilly detained persons may not view the justice system as a legitimate or respected institution—a belief that is associated with increased recidivism (Dorsett 1998). There are also ethical considerations for society at large. If the notion spreads that someone can be committed for "who they are" (that is, as someone *believed* to be dangerous in the future), society may lose the ability to compel law-abiding behavior. Additionally, people may lose the desire and incentive to comply with rules and regulations. As discussed in earlier sections, despite recent advancements in actuarial methods, the complexity of human behavior makes accurate assessments of what someone will do in the future extremely difficult—particularly with low base rate events, like some sex crimes.

Another implication of civil commitment statutes is the increased cost to the justice and forensic mental health systems. The state of Washington reports that it costs approximately $92,000 a year to house a sex offender under this statute (La Fond 1998). This is more than twice the sum of an annual incarceration in a prison facility. Likewise, the state of Minnesota reports that it will spend nearly $20 million per year to commit approximately 10 percent of the state's convicted sex offender population. This figure is expected to triple by the year 2010 (Janus 2003). During this same period the state allocated only $1.1 million to fund community-based sex offender treatment for over 900 probationers, as well as 450 post-release offenders, and $2.1 million per year to treat over 1,200 incarcerated sex offenders (Janus 2003). In the final analysis, civil commitment of sex offenders consumes over 85 percent of the state's annual correctional treatment budget (Janus 2003). The expenditure to civilly commit a small portion of sex offenders is so great that programs targeting much larger correctional sex offender populations are "under-funded and under-developed" (Janus 2003, 7). Not only are these costs extraordinary high on a per offender basis, but states that have adopted civil commitment statutes are finding that many more offenders are being committed than ever expected. For instance, in 1994 when Wisconsin passed its civil commitment legislation, it was assumed only seven or eight offenders would be committed annually. Within five years, however, more than one hundred (not the expected forty-five) offenders have been civilly committed under the sexual predator law, and nearly as many cases are awaiting disposition (Friedland 1999). Despite these high costs, many of the facilities used to house committed sex offenders offer either substandard treatment or no therapeutic intervention at all (Friedland 1999). Given that sex offender treatment produces measurable—and at times dramatic—reductions in sexual recidivism, critical reviewers of public policy must question whether expensive sexual predator laws are worth the consumption of scarce money and resources.

In conclusion, because of ethical concerns, the potential for misuse and abuse of civil commitment statutes (Lieb et al. 1998), and the drain on resources for preventive detention to both the criminal justice and forensic mental health systems, it is evident that civil commitment statutes not be the policy of choice to deal with high-risk sex offenders (Friedland 1999). Rather, a more prudent policy is to encourage and systemically support conventional criminal sanctions to be used properly. Accurate offense charging and a genuine commitment to imposing appropriate criminal sentences (which means, among other things, reducing the pressure on state's attorneys to process cases quickly) are more efficacious judicial responses to serious offenders than preventive detention. In instances where it is appropriate, sex offenders should be sentenced to sufficiently long prison terms and not be permitted to avoid severe legal sanctions. Had this protocol been followed, the child killers associated with the advent of the third wave of sex offender legislation might still have been incarcerated at the time they sexually assaulted and murdered their victims. In addition, making sex offender treatment available to inmates during the term of their incarceration will amount to merely a blip on the Department of Correction budget sheet compared to the costs of civil commitment (Friedland 1999).

In this chapter I put sex offender laws into historical context to provide the reader with the myriad of concerns, perspectives, and fears that pervade the social policy responses to sexual violence. In so doing, I conducted a critical probe into the likely impact of these legislative initiatives. Unfortunately, limited empirical data on sex offender legislation leaves many unanswered questions about the impact of these social policies. The required "guesswork" as to the ultimate effect these laws have on community safety is particularly disturbing, considering that 60 percent of all convicted sexual offenders are being supervised in a communal setting via probation or parole (Greenfeld 1997). Thus, in the following chapters I shall provide analyses of a group of male sex offenders ordered to serve their sentences under community-based supervision. This population was studied to learn the extent to which these men recidivated while under the jurisdiction of the court and the watchful eyes of probation agents, surveillance officers, and forensic therapists. In addition, I collected data on their perceptions of sex offender laws and many issues of relevance to their crimes, as well as their self-reported projections of their own future sexual violence.

Sex Offenders in Your Backyard

Although exceptions exist [with regard to rape of college co-eds], most sexual victimizations occur when college women are alone with a man they know, at night, and in the privacy of a residence.

—Fisher, Cullen and Turner 2000, 16.

U p to this point I have discussed several topics relevant to sex offenders: how they come to know their victims, how the media and criminal justice system respond to sex crimes, what the recidivism rate is among this population of criminals, what treatment interventions show promise; I have also provided an introduction to the various types of sex offender legislation. The tone and content of this chapter are different: the focus shifts away from the larger sociological discussion we have been having thus far on sex offenders and their crimes in favor of a microlevel analysis (involving probation files within a specialized sex offender unit and interviews with convicted sex offenders) on a specific population of men convicted of sex crimes who were sentenced to probation in a large suburban county (approximate population 650,000) in the middle region of the country.

As noted earlier, the use of probation and parole as a sentencing option for sex offenders has become increasingly common. As such the performance of a population of sex offenders on probation is of primary interest here. To that end I shall introduce the specialized sex offender probation unit that was responsible for overseeing the community supervision of the men included in this specific study and discuss the types of sex crimes that lead to their convictions. Personal information about the offenders and their victims and the significant findings associated with the recidivism portion of the study is covered. Specifically, results from this investigation indicate that 12 percent of the probationers committed a new sex crime during the course of community supervision and that sex offenders who assaulted strangers and probationers who indicated they had been sexually abused in the past were the most dangerous sex offenders on probation. Although quantitative research, as is covered in this chapter, can be challenging to read and comprehend it enhances our understanding of sex offender recidivism because it identifies which factors are most predictive of sexual reoffending and how variables interact with one another. This probe into the probation files of convicted sex offenders and the subsequent interviews with a sampling of these men (chapter 5) are critical to increasing what is known about the activities of sex offenders on probation and determining whether the criminal justice system should be using community-based sanctions on convicted sex criminals.

SEX OFFENDER PROBATION

In 1996 the Midwestern suburb where these data were eventually collected became one of the first probation departments in the country to specialize in sex offender supervision with a self-declared mission of "no more victims." The probation department became the central component to a collaborative effort among law enforcement, the courts, and the therapeutic community to effectively and safely supervise sex offenders serving a criminal sentence in the community. Over the next several years these practices evolved into what came to be known as the *containment approach* to sex offender supervision (Center for Sex Offender Management 2002; English et al. 1996). Generally, the containment approach to sex offender management involves three central elements: (1) offenders are taught how to attain internal control of their impulses, behaviors, and feelings; (2), the criminal justice system provides social control measures through the use of sanctions and conditions (for example, intensive supervision, mandatory treatment, denying contact with minors or victims); and (3) the use of polygraph examinations to monitor the offender's overall compliance with treatment and probation conditions. Prior to the commencement of this research the probation department secured state and federal funding to support their innovative supervision techniques of sex offenders. The unit employs six probation and two surveillance officers. Each specialized caseload is limited to forty-five sex offenders per officer. I gained entrée to this population of sex offenders, in part, because I had previously been employed as a probation officer with the agency. Also, they granted rare research access because the department is dedicated to improving their services and enhancing public safety, and the outcome of studies like this helps determine the best way to respond to these offenders.

The data utilized for this component of the study were obtained by examining the probation and court files of all adult men[1] who were convicted of sex crimes and who were actively on probation and had been supervised by the sex offender unit for at least six months[2] ($n = 169$). I had access to the offender's criminal record, employment and residential information, probation progress and violation reports, clinical evaluations and treatment notes, polygraph examination results, and supervision case notes, among other things. Community-based supervision requirements for this group of offenders *minimally* included weekly or biweekly probation appointments, monthly scheduled and unscheduled home visits by probation agents and surveillance officers, collateral contacts, mandated therapeutic intervention, no-victim-contact and/or no-contact-with-minors court orders, drug and alcohol screening, DNA/STD/HIV testing, and community notification for offenders who were convicted of charges that mandated registration.

LIMITATIONS TO PROBATION RESEARCH

There are inevitably limitations to every study and this one is no exception. Despite the multitude of sources that were referenced to detect sexual recidivism, it is possible that these men committed additional sex crimes while on probation that were not reported by the victim or discovered by law enforcement, probation agents, or clinicians. The second limitation to the quantitative portion of the research pertains to the deterrence and rational choice theory–testing portion of the study. It assumes that the objective reality of certainty, severity, and celerity of sanctions and the offenders' perception of these factors are one and the same, but in reality there is no way to ensure that they are. Additionally, the test of deterrence focuses primarily on the "costs" (offenders' assessments of sanctions) associated with crime, not the "benefit" (offenders' perceptions of enjoyment associated with the act) side of the equation, so it is not a complete test of the theory.[3] Third, the validity of self-reported information is questionable and one of the two significant findings contained in the regression model—sexual victimization in the offender's past—was based on self-report data. The accuracy of these self-reports may be further compromised in that the reports were provided by convicted sex offenders, a group of criminals notorious for misrepresenting facts and trying to present themselves in a more favorable light (Scully 1994). Fourth, logistic regression was performed on these data to determine the relationship between the dependent variable (sexual recidivism) and each of the independent variables (factors believed to predict sexual reoffending) while statistically controlling for the other variables in the model. To accomplish this task, only files with no missing data in any of the categories were available for final analysis. This means that the available sample size dropped from 169 cases to 101 probation files. Finally, as noted in chapter 2, recidivism studies on sexual violence are plagued with low base rates, which occur when the phenomenon under study is a rare event. From a safety vantage point it is good news that most sex offenders do not appear to recidivate. In this case, only 20 of the 169 men in this study committed a new sex crime while under intensive supervision by the courts and probation. From a research perspective, however, less information available for review (only twenty cases available for close recidivism examination) makes predictions of future behavior and unearthing new information more difficult.

SEX CRIMES AND THEIR VICTIMS

The men on probation in this unit were convicted or pleaded guilty to an array of sex crimes. The majority of them were currently on probation for felony sex offenses (aggravated criminal assault, predatory criminal sexual assault, child pornography, and sexual exploitation of a child). About 40 of the 169 sex offenders, however, had misdemeanor sex crime convictions such as public indecency, solicitation, criminal sexual abuse, and Internet-related sex charges. Consistent with previous literature, nearly all of the victims in this investigation (80 percent) knew their offenders prior to the commission of the sex crime. In fact, the vast majority were friends or family members of the offenders. The youngest victim was three years of age at the time of the crime and the eldest was sixty. The average victim age was fifteen. Nearly 75 percent of these victims were female and almost half of the victimizations (49 percent) involved a violation of trust of the victim-offender relationship. In this study, the violation of trust by an offender was operationalized to mean the sexual victimizer was a parent, relative, teacher, religious leader, or coach to the victim.

THE SEX OFFENDERS

Table 4.1 displays sociodemographic characteristics and offense history features, as well as sanctions and treatment/behavioral conditions imposed by the court for this group of sex offender probationers. As shown, the average age of this sex offender population is thirty-four. About three-quarters of the men are white and the majority are not married. In addition, more than half of these male sex offenders have completed high school or attended college, which is rare among generalized (non-sex-offending) criminal populations. The majority of the men did not change their primary residence in the twelve months preceding this study. Only 16 percent of the offenders have previous felony convictions of any kind—a sharp contrast to the populations included in most sex offender recidivism studies, which tend to be composed primarily of ex-felons.

Formal "Costs" of Sex Offenses

Part of the deterrence and rational choice model involves personal calculations of the "costs" (formal and informal sanctions) associated with being caught for a criminal act. In this study the formal "costs" started with an average two and a half year probation sentence (thirty months) in a specialized sex offender unit. Also, 70 percent of the sex offenders in this study were legally required to register with local law enforcement as convicted sex offenders and were similarly subjected to community notification. Less than half of these men were ordered to serve time in jail as a condition of their probation. The overwhelming majority (80 percent) of sex offenders studied here were monitored under maximum-supervision contact standards, which mandated that they meet frequently with their probation officer in the office and at their residence. They were also visited on a regular basis by the surveillance officers and required to attend specialized sex offender therapy. The officers required collateral verification (residence, employment, victim restitution payments, and so forth) from the offenders on a weekly or biweekly basis and constantly monitored their treatment and compliance status. On average, the sex offenders were

Table 4.1

Demographic Characteristics, Offense History, Court Sanctions, and Treatment/ Behavioral Conditions Features (n = 169)

	% of total		% of total
Age distribution (mean=34)		No. of times relocated	
18 to 23	23.5	No moves	64.5
24 to 29	16.2	One move	26.2
30 to 35	17.4	Two or more moves	9.2
36 to 41	20.4	Maximum supervision	
42 or older	22.5	No	17.9
Race		Yes	82.1
White	72.2	Felony history	
Non-white	27.8	No prior felonies	84.1
Marital status		One or more prior felonies	15.9
Single	58.5		
Married/cohabitating	41.5	Jail time imposed	
Education level		No	60.1
Grade school	4.8	Yes	39.9
Some high school	29.7	Registered as a sex offender	
High school/GED	41.1		
Some college	16	No	30.3
College or graduate degree	8.4	Yes	69.7
Victim-offender relationship		Employment (in months)*	9.1 (4.5)
Family or friend to victim	79.0		
Stranger to victim	21.0		
Offender's self-reported prior victimization		No. of behavioral conditions imposed by the courts*	2.83 (1.79)
No	72.4		
Yes	27.6	Length of probation sentence (in months)*	29.61 (16.45)

Note: *Mean of valid cases; standard deviation is shown in parentheses.

mandated to complete about three different treatment conditions successfully. Furthermore, records from the probation department indicate that, on average, sex offenders were ordered to comply with more behavioral treatment conditions than non–sex offender probation clients. Also, the frequency of contact with probation personnel and the length of contact on a per visit basis is twice that of probationers on general supervision caseloads.

THE IMPACT OF OFFENDER DEMOGRAPHICS, INFORMAL SOCIAL CONTROLS, AND LEGAL SANCTIONS ON SEXUAL RECIDIVISM

Prior to discussing the regression analysis, it is important to determine first the bivariate relationships among the dependent variable (sexual recidivism) and the independent variables (offender and offense attributes, extralegal social controls, legal "costs" of committing a sex offense, and situational constraints on behavior). Table 4.2 displays these percentage distributions for the categorical independent variables believed to be associated with sexual recidivism. At the bivariate level, there is only one independent variable that happens to be a formal social control measure significantly correlated with sexual recidivism: jail sentence imposed as a condition of probation. More specifically, 17.7 percent of the sex offenders who received a jail sentence as a condition of probation sexually recidivated while only 5.6 percent of the men who did not receive a jail term as part of their community-based supervision committed a new sex offense while under the court's jurisdiction. In a higher level of analysis, other studies have indicated that jail time (as a condition of community-based supervision) is statistically significant and predictive of sexual recidivism among felony sex offender probationers (Meloy 2005). The positive relationship between incarceration (as a condition of probation) and increased sexual recidivism is perhaps explained by the fact that especially serious sex offenders are the ones most likely to be required to serve jail time. These men are also the offenders we would expect to pose the greatest risk to community safety. This finding may suggest that there is a subsample of sex offender probationers currently receiving community-based sentences who are too dangerous for this type of sanction.

Additionally, as can be seen in Table 4.2, although not statistically meaningful, the following relationships emerged: younger sex offenders, those aged 24 to 29, recidivated at a higher rate (29.2 percent) than the oldest group of sex offenders (10.4 percent); a higher percentage of non-white offenders sexually recidivated (18.6 percent) than white offenders (10.1 percent); sex offenders with a high school degree (or equivalency) recidivated more often (18.2 percent) than sex offenders who had the highest levels of education (7.1 percent); sex offenders who were single or living alone were more likely to sexually recidivate (15.6 percent) during probation than the sex offenders who were married or cohabiting with a partner (7.5 percent); sex offenders with children recidivated sexually dur-

Table 4.2

Bivariate Relationship in Percentages between the Categorical Independent Variables and Sexual Recidivism

Predictors	Did not sexually recidivate	Sexually recidivated
Offender's age (cramer's $v = .21, p > .05$		
18 to 23	91.4% ($n = 32$)	8.6% ($n = 3$)
24 to 29	70.8% ($n = 17$)	29.2% ($n = 7$)
30 to 35	91.7% ($n = 22$)	8.3% ($n = 2$)
36 to 41	89.3% ($n = 25$)	10.7% ($n = 3$)
42 or older	89.6% ($n = 43$)	10.4% ($n = 5$)
Race (phi $= .11, p > .05$)		
Non-white	81.4% ($n = 35$)	18.6% ($n = 8$)
White	89.9% ($n = 107$)	10.1% ($n = 12$)
Education level (cramer's $v = .15$, $p > .05$)		
Grade school	100% ($n = 7$)	0% ($n = 0$)
Some high school	87.8% ($n = 43$)	12.2% ($n = 6$)
High school or GED	81.8% ($n = 54$)	18.2% ($n = 12$)
Some college	96.2% ($n = 25$)	3.8% ($n = 1$)
College or graduate degree	92.9% ($n = 13$)	7.1% ($n = 1$)
Married/cohabitating (phi $= -.12$, $p > .05$)		
Married/cohabitating	92.5% ($n = 62$)	7.5% ($n = 5$)
Not married	84.4% ($n = 76$)	15.6% ($n = 14$)
Parental status (phi $= .01, p > .05$)		
Has one or more children	86.7% ($n = 72$)	13.3% ($n = 11$)
Has no children	87.8% ($n = 65$)	12.2% ($n = 9$)
Stable employment (phi $= -.04$, $p > .05$)		
Employed at least 6 months	92.0% ($n = 104$)	8.0% ($n = 9$)
Employed less than 6 months	88.9% ($n = 24$)	11.1% ($n = 3$)
Residential stability (cramer's $v = .19$, $p > .05$)		
No moves	94.5% ($n = 86$)	5.5% ($n = 5$)
One move	83.8% ($n = 31$)	16% ($n = 6$)
Two or more moves	100% ($n = 12$)	0% ($n = 0$)
Victim-offender relationship (phi $= .01, p > .05$)		
Offender was a stranger	86.7% ($n = 26$)	13.3% ($n = 4$)
Offender knew the victim	88.2% ($n = 97$)	11.8% ($n = 13$)

Table 4.2 *(continued)*

Predictors	Did not sexually recidivate	Sexually recidivated
Victimization of offender (phi = .12, $p > .05$)		
Prior victimization/abuse	82.2% ($n = 37$)	17.8% ($n = 8$)
No history of victimization	91.1% ($n = 102$)	8.9% ($n = 8$)
Prior felony convictions		
One or more felonies	80.8% ($n = 21$)	19.2% ($n = 5$)
No prior record	90.9% ($n = 120$)	9.1% ($n = 12$)
*Jail sentence (phi = .19, $p < .01$)		
Received jail sentence	82.3% ($n = 51$)	17.7% ($n = 11$)
Probation only	94.4% ($n = 84$)	5.6% ($n = 5$)

*$p < .01$

ing their probation term more often (13.3 percent) than sex offenders with no children (12.2 percent); sex offenders who were employed for fewer than six months of the year recidivated more often (11.1 percent) than sex offenders who were employed for additional months (8.0 percent); and sex offenders on probation who moved once during the previous year committed new sex crimes more often (16 percent) than the probationers who did not change their primary residence (5.5 percent).

Other nonsignificant statistical bivariate relationships found that offenders who victimized strangers were more likely to sexually recidivate (13.3 percent) than sex offenders who victimized a family member or acquaintance (11.8 percent). Also, offenders with their own history of childhood victimization were more likely to sexually recidivate during a term of probation (17.8 percent) than were the sex offenders in the sample who were not victimized as children (8.9 percent). Finally, sex offenders with prior felony convictions were more likely to commit a new sex crime while on probation (19.2 percent) than were probationers with no prior convictions (9.1 percent).

To recap, at the bivariate level, there was only one independent variable (imposition of a jail sentence) that was statistically predictive of sexual recidivism during probation. This factor was identified as a way to measure the impact of formal social controls on future offending behavior; that is, when examining the relationship between the independent events of sexual recidivism during probation and the imposition of a jail sentence, a meaningful and positive association exists between the two. The association between these factors is likely the result of more serious offenders' (and hence those most likely to recidivate) receiving jail terms as part of probation. Researchers and policymakers should seriously question whether sex offenders who "deserve" jail time should be eligible for probation. The other associations discussed in this section were statistically nonsignificant; that is, it is unclear if the outcomes are real or caused by chance.

Sexual Recidivism Results

A review of the data indicates that 20 of the 169 (roughly 12 percent) sex offenders included in this study sexually recidivated during the term of their community-based supervision. This rate of reoffending is consistent with that of documented recidivism rates for collapsed samples (that is, heterogeneous) of sex offenders (Hanson and Bussiere 1998; Greenfeld 1997; Langan et al. 2003). Where it is higher than comparison samples of sex offenders on probation (Kruttschnitt et al. 2000; Meloy 2005), it is likely attributed to the broad definition of recidivism and comprehensiveness of data sources available to uncover additional sex crimes. Research demonstrates that an increase in community surveillance intensity is associated with a corresponding increase in the detection of infractions and violations (Petersilia and Turner 1993). On average, it took eight months of a probation term for these sex offenders to commit a new sex crime. Within sixteen months all but two of the twenty recidivists had committed a new sex crime. This suggests that there is a time frame when sex offender probationers are most at risk to recidivate sexually. Particular attention should be paid to offenders during this period in their community supervision to help decrease reoffending. The heightened risk period may suggest that eight to sixteen months allows ample time-to-offend (that is, the number of days offenders are on the street). Or it may be indicative of something else, such as critical periods in the offender's community supervision (all facets of intensive probation surveillance are in full effect), or the treatment process (offenders may be dealing with emotionally charged issues that make them especially vulnerable to reoffend). In addition, significant dynamic (changing) risk factors—such as housing, employment, and avoidance of substance abuse—may be negatively impacted (by community notification or the like) at this time. Without additional information it is impossible to know for certain what explains this risky period in an offender's probation term.

As mentioned earlier, logistic regression is utilized to assess the effects of each of the independent variables (factors believed to be associated with sexual reoffending) on the dependent variable (sexual reoffense), while simultaneously controlling for the other factors included in the model. Overall, there were two variables (stranger assailants and self-reported prior victimization of the offender) that were predictive of sexual recidivism during probation, while controlling for the other factors in the model. Table 4.3 provides a chart summation of the results of the regression analysis for sexual recidivism. Appendix A provides a complete coding summary for all of the variables included in the regression analysis.

Offender Demographics and Offense History

Offender demographics, such as age and race, are typically strong indicators of criminal reoffending (Nagin, Farrington, and Moffitt 1995), and, as such, are included in the logistic regression model. Although the relationship is not statistically significant here, age is negatively related to recidivism when controlling for the other variables in the model ($B = -.043; p > .05$). In other words, older sex offenders are less likely to sexually recidivate than are younger sex offenders but the relationship is not

Table 4.3

Unstandardized Regression Coefficients for Sexual Recidivism among Adult Male Sex Offenders ($n = 101$)

	B	Std. Error	Wald	Exp(B)
Age	-.043	.055	.6165	.957
Race	-.218	1.511	.0209	.803
Education	-.259	.205	1.5896	.771
Marital status	-.847	1.728	.240	.428
Parental status	1.605	1.408	1.298	4.979
Employment	8.706	36.856	.055	6.044+ 3
Residential instability	.402	.7073	.3232	1.495
Offender was a stranger	2.895*	1.365	4.495	18.093
Victimization of offender	2.176*	1.123	3.751	8.818
Prior felony convictions	-.394	1.613	.0596	.674
Jail sentence	2.409	1.325	3.303	11.128
Treatment conditions	.186	.352	.280	1.205
Constant	-11.341	36.934	.094	
χ^2	15.435	$df = 12$		

$^*p < .05$

statistically meaningful. Once again, although not statistically significant, race of offender is negatively related to sexual recidivism after considering the effects of the other variables in the model ($B = -.218; p > .05$). Simply stated, non-white sex offenders are less likely to recidivate than their white counterparts. The bivariate findings indicate that eight non-white offenders recidivated while twelve white sex offenders committed a new sex crime during the course of probation. Because there was no statistical significance associated with this regression outcome, however, it is meaningless from a mathematical standpoint.

Similarly, previous research indicates an inverse relationship between years of education and involvement in crime and deviance; therefore, educational attainment is also included in the model (Shover and Thompson 1992). The results here indicate that additional years of education has a nonsignificant and inverse relationship with sexual recidivism, after controlling for the other effects in the model ($B = -.259; p > .05$). In other words, sex offenders with additional years of education are less likely to sexually recidivate but it cannot be determined if this relationship is real or caused by chance.

Empirical data suggest that prior physical, sexual, and/or emotional victimization in the offender's childhood is correlated with higher rates of sexual violence. Roughly one-third of all sex offenders report they experienced some level of victimization in their past (Heilbrun et al. 1998), which is an overrepresentation among males in the general population. Therefore, the defendants' self-reported prior victimization is included in the model. The relationship between childhood victimization and adult sex offending behavior is born out here. Regression results indicate that the defendant's self-reported prior childhood abuse appears to be a strong indicator of future sexual violence; defendant's prior victimization is positively correlated and statistically significant even when controlling for the other variables in the model ($B = 2.17; p < .05$). In fact, the odds that a defendant who reports childhood victimization will recidivate is about 8.81 times greater than for defendants who do not report victimization in their past.

Additionally, studies of sexual violence consistently indicate that sex offenders who victimize strangers have a greater propensity to reoffend than offenders who victimize someone they know (Berliner et al. 1995; Hanson and Bussiere 1998; Terry 2006). To assess the impact of relationship context on sexual reoffending, victim-offender-relationships are included in the model. The stranger-assailants in this study also proved to be more dangerous than other types of sex offenders. Findings indicate that the relationship between victims and offenders is positively correlated and statistically significant when considering the other effects in the model ($B = 2.89$; $p < .05$). Specifically, offenders who sexually assaulted strangers are more likely to sexually recidivate while on probation than offenders who knew their victims. In fact, the odds that a stranger-assailant will recidivate while under the court's supervision is about eighteen times greater than for offenders who were friends or family members of their victims.

One of the strongest predictors of future criminal activity is prior felony convictions (Barbaree and Marshall 1988). In this study, however, prior felony convictions are nonsignificant and inversely related to sexual recidivism when controlling for the other effects in the model ($B = -.394$; $p > .05$). Recall that less than 20 percent of the population was known to have a prior felony conviction and that the bivariate results indicate that 80 percent of the sex offenders with a prior felony conviction did *not* sexually recidivate while on probation—which could explain the inverse relationship associated with this finding. Only five of twenty-six sex offenders with one or more known prior felonies sexually recidivated while under the court's supervision. Also, because the outcome related to prior felony arrests did not meet the criteria to be statistically meaningful (that is, 95 percent certainty that it was an accurate representation of the relationship between these factors and not occurring by chance) we cannot speak with authority about what this finding means because it may simply have occurred at random.

Informal Social Controls

Research findings indicate that extralegal factors often have a stronger deterrent effect on criminal behavior than formal legal sanctions (Laub, Nagin, and Sampson 1998). Therefore, probationers' marital status and if the offender had children were included as gauges of informal social control. The regression results indicate that marital status has a nonsignificant and negative relationship with sexual recidivism when controlling for the other effects in the model ($B = -.847$; $p > .05$). Sex offenders who are married or cohabitating are less likely to recidivate than their single counterparts but there is no statistical importance related to this outcome.

Whether or not defendants have children is positively correlated with sexual recidivism but not statistically significant. This finding suggests that sex offenders who have children are more likely to sexually recidivate even after considering the other effects in the regression model ($B = 1.605$; $p > .05$). Readers should recall from table 4.2, however, that the differences between recidivists with children ($n = 11$) and recidivists without children ($n = 9$) was minor and not statistically significant. Theoretically speaking, this finding was a surprise; it had been assumed that children would act as informal social control agents and would deter additional sex crimes by their sex-offending fathers. Assuming that this result is representative of an actual relationship (and did not occur randomly), a plausible explanation for the lack of deterrence with regard to this informal social control is that the offenders were not residing with their children during the period of their community supervision. This separation may have occurred because they had previously victimized their children (incest offense) and were therefore denied any further contact or that they were simply barred from cohabiting with minors as a general safety precaution. Another possible explanation is that recidivists assaulted their own children. Given the lack of statistical significance, it is unknown if this finding is "real" or a coincidence.

In addition, employment stability has been shown to be correlated with a reduced probability of reoffending among sex offenders[4] (Kruttschnitt et al. 2000) and is used as another measure of the impact of informal social controls. Regression analysis results indicate a positive but nonsignificant relationship between recidivism and employment even after considering the other effects in the model ($B = 8.706$; $p > .5$). As defendants gain additional months of employment, they are more likely to sexually recidivate than defendants who do not gain additional months of employment. The directional relationship between employment and sexual recidivism is contrary to extant literature. Given that this outcome is statistically insignificant, it may have resulted by chance alone. Further, if employment stability had been measured in number of employers in the previous year rather than in the number of months employed in the previous year, the relationship direction may have been different and more consistent with other empirical data. Also, it is important to note at the bivariate level of analysis, 92 percent of the sex offender population with more than six months employment did *not* sexually recidivate.

Previous research also links community integration and stability with lower recidivism rates (Bellair 1997). To examine the effect of this informal social control variable on sexual recidivism, the frequency with which the defendant moved in the last twelve months was also included in the model. Although the relationship is not statistically significant, residential instability is positively correlated with sexual recidivism after controlling for the other effects in the regression model ($B = .402; p > .05$). In other words, sex offenders who move frequently are more likely to recidivate than sex offenders who maintain the same residence. Still, caution must be exercised when interpreting this finding because the outcome did not reach the threshold of statistical significance.

Formal Legal Sanctions

An inverse relationship between certainty and severity of formal legal sanctions and criminality is implied in our criminal justice system and is an integral component to the deterrence/rational choice theory. As such, the requirement of a jail sentence as part of probation and the number of mandated treatment conditions are both included as proxies for measures of formal social control. Mandated treatment conditions often include some combination of (1) individual therapy sessions; (2) group therapy sessions; (3) drug or alcohol restrictions and/or substance abuse treatment; (4) no contact orders with minors or victims; (5) driving restrictions; (6) aversion therapy techniques; (7) mandatory polygraph testing or other objective testing measures; and (8) pharmacological intervention.[5]

A jail sentence imposed as a condition of probation positively influences sexual recidivism when controlling for the other effects in the model, but the outcome is not statistically meaningful ($B = 2.40; p > .05$). The interpretation of this finding suggests that when sex offenders receive a sentence of probation that includes jail time, the offender is more likely to recidivate than those sex offenders who are not sentenced to a period of incarceration regardless of all other factors. The odds that a sex offender will sexually recidivate if he is ordered to serve a period of incarceration is approximately eleven times higher than a sex offender for whom jail was not imposed. Despite the dramatic increase in odds among sex offenders who recidivated and were ordered to serve jail time, the relationship did not meet or exceed the criteria necessary to be statistically significant (which means the outcome could be due to chance). Recall that the relationship between jail time and recidivism was significant at the bivariate level but the statistical relationship was not maintained when the other variables in the regression model were considered.

Finally, the number of treatment conditions imposed as a condition of probation is also positively related to sexual recidivism (but not statistically significant) after considering the effects of the other variables in the model ($B = .186; p > .05$). Deterrence and rational choice models of crime predict that reoffending behavior decreases as "costs" (in this case in the form of additional treatment conditions) increase. In this particular case the likelihood of recidivism actually increased (not decreased) along with additional units in treatment conditions, although the outcome was not statistically important. If this finding reflects an actual positive relationship, perhaps offenders felt overwhelmed by the additional treatment conditions and gave up on the possibility of being successful on probation. Perhaps additional treatment conditions actually did reduce recidivism in terms of how quickly probationers failed or how many victims they had, but their therapeutic and/or formal social control impact was not fully detected. In the absence of a statistically influential outcome on the relationship between treatment conditions and sex offender probationers it is not possible to know the short-term recidivism effects of adding treatment and behavioral conditions to community supervision. More study is desperately needed.

At first blush, these last two findings seem to contradict that portion of the specific deterrence theory which suggests the greater the "costs" associated with a crime (jail time versus no jail time and additional treatment mandates on probation compared to fewer requirements) the less inclined offenders will be to engage in more crime. Remember, these are statistically nonsignificant results so we cannot be certain what caused their outcome. For example, if incarceration as a term of probation truly is predictive of sexual recidivism, perhaps what we are really measuring is an indication of dangerousness. The courts are more inclined to require additional punitive sanctions on offenders who have committed more serious crimes and/or have lengthier criminal histories. The positive relationship between sexual recidivism and jail sentences and additional units of treatment (albeit statistically nonsignificant) should be further evaluated to determine if these factors can be predictive of increased risk of sexual reoffending during probation. If a significant relationship is established—as it has been elsewhere—we may postulate that there may be a segment of the sex offender probation population that is too high-risk for community-based supervision even with the use of extrapunitive sanctions.

As indicated by the Wald statistic (see table 4.3), the independent variable stranger-assailant, has the strongest influence on sexual recidivism during probation followed by defendants' prior victimization and jail sentenced imposed as a condition of probation. Similarly, the Wald statistic indicates the variables of least importance in the model are race, stability of employment and prior felony record. Finally, the Chi-Square statistic ($\chi^2 = 15.435$; $p > .05$; $df = 12$) indicates that the model is not a good fit to the data. Still, with statistical adjustments, this combination of variables accurately identified 87 percent of the sex offenders on community-based supervision who sexually recidivated during a term of probation.[6] This result is an improvement over some predictive instruments used by the criminal justice system.

In this chapter I have discussed the sexual recidivism rate that occurred during probation, provided a personal and criminal history profile of the sex offender population studied here, and outlined the statistical predictors of committing a new sex crime during the course of community-based supervision. I determined that 12 percent of the probationers committed a new sex crime while on community-based supervision and that men who sexually violated strangers (persons unknown or barely known to them) and those men who reported they were the victims of childhood abuse were the most dangerous offenders on probation. These findings suggest that offense (victim-offender relationships) and offender attributes (childhood victimization) were more influential in this instance in predicting future dangerousness among sex offender probationers than formal and informal social controls or situational factors. It is important to keep this recidivism finding in perspective: 88 percent of the sex offenders whose activities and behaviors were heavily scrutinized by the agents in this specialized unit did *not* reoffend during their community-based supervision. It is significantly less expensive, per year, to place an offender on probation (assuming probationers do not commit new crimes or create new victims) than it is to incarcerate him. Furthermore, some evidence even suggests that sex offender probationers recidivate *less* often than those sentenced to prison (Langan, Schmitt, and Durose 2003; Meloy 2005). Not only is there potential cost savings and reductions in reoffending associated with placing low risk sex offenders on probation (in lieu of prison), but these clients are also more likely to receive sex offender treatment opportunities than incarcerated offenders (Center for Sex Offender Management 2002; Turner, Bingham, and Andrasik 2000). Recall that much research tells us that treatment further reduces the risk of both general and sexual recidivism (Alexander 1999; Hanson 2000a).

So what policy lessons can we take from this? Researchers, lawmakers, and criminal justice personnel have the difficult task to make informed decisions (that is, those grounded in science) regarding which candidates should receive specialized community-based sanctions and where funding should be allocated (or re-allocated from prison budgets if necessary) to ensure probation departments are adequately staffed with personnel specifically trained to work with sex offenders. Additionally, appropriate community-based treatment must be available with clinician providers willing to work closely with judicial and law enforcement personnel. Keep in mind, based on outcomes here and elsewhere there are policy-relevant issues such as the relationship between the imposition of jail time as a condition of probation and future offending behavior that should be further evaluated. Chapter 5 builds on these recidivism findings by augmenting interview data from a smaller group of the sex offenders who were on probation at the time this study was conducted.

Sex Offenders Speak Out

Sex offender registration and community notification makes
you feel like a total outcast. It makes me feel like a piece of dirt.
This label, it makes me feel as if I am already dead.

—As stated by a convicted sex offender
in 1997; Meloy 2000b: 20.

I report here on the significant findings related to the interviews conducted with some of the sex offenders on probation. Subjects were
questioned about their experiences with the criminal justice system
and asked to speculate about the impact of sex offender laws and official
protocol designed to deter sexual violence. Moreover, to develop a more
comprehensive understanding of the decision-making processes of sexually violent men, I questioned respondents about several topics related to
their own acts of violence. With respect to the in-depth interviews, six primary themes emerged from an analysis of the data; each will be discussed
subsequently.

SEX OFFENDER INTERVIEWS

This portion of the study was designed to build upon the statistical findings generated from the probation files. The offenders' own words and
perceptions may teach us a great deal about their behavior; also, studying sexual violence from a nonquantitative approach may overcome some
of the inherent obstacles associated with low base rate events (see chapter 4). How an individual defines a situation is central to how that individual behaves. Therefore, how these offenders perceive and understand
the potential risks and pleasures associated with sexual violence, and the
criminal justice system's response to their crimes can have direct implica-

tions on their decisions to offend or desist from offending. Of the 169 eligible defendants on probation at the time the study was conducted, 29 offenders agreed to be interviewed for this study.

Participation in the interview component of the study was strictly voluntary. Subjects were advised that this was academic research and were assured that the project had nothing whatsoever to do with their probation status. In other words, they were repeatedly advised that they would not be rewarded or given any special favors or accommodations by their probation officer if they agreed to talk with me. Similarly, the men were not coerced, threatened, or punished in any way for deciding not to participate in the interview portion of the study. Subjects who volunteered to be interviewed were presented with a copy of (and read aloud) a University-approved Internal Review Board informed consent stipulating the research goals and potential benefits and risks associated with participation. Interview times ranged from thirty minutes to two and a half hours with most interviews averaging about one and a half hours in length. The discussions with offenders were followed by a deterrence/rational choice survey depicting a hypothetical sexual assault scenario where offenders were asked to assess the "costs" versus "benefits" of engaging in the sex crime depicted in the scenario. Unfortunately, this portion of the study failed to produce any significant findings because there was virtually no variability in the dependent variable: that is, nearly every offender who took the survey stated that he would not be likely to engage in any additional sex crimes.

A structured research instrument was used in the interview process (see appendix B). Nevertheless, the interview portion of the study was guided by grounded theory (Glaser and Strauss 1967).[1] Each interview was unique. For example, although the interviews were semistructured, participants were strongly encouraged to raise and discuss topics of importance to them and their experience with the criminal justice system that went beyond the confines of the designed research instrument. Essentially, grounded theory was used to explore how community-based supervision impacted the lives of these twenty-nine convicted offenders as well as what they had to say about the criminal justice system's response to sexual violence. All of the interviews were taped and transcribed verbatim. Rather than concentrating on line-by-line coding, the qualitative analysis involved identifying core themes and categories that emerged from multiple reads of the interview data (Rubin and Rubin 1995; Strauss and Corbin 1998). This process was continued until the point of saturation was reached (Strauss and

Corbin 1998). Finally, to ensure the confidentiality of all respondents, pseudonyms are always used when referring to research subjects.

Limitations to the Interviews

It is well documented that sex offenders suffer from varying degrees of cognitive distortions (Hanson and Bussiere 1998; Hanson, Scott, and Steffy 1995; Salter 2003). As such, discrepancies between actual events and the construction (or reconstruction) of events from an offender's perspective is common. Certainly, this re-creating must be considered when evaluating the words and thoughts of this group. Not only do sex offenders often suffer from cognitive distortions, they are prone to manipulate or lie to help form favorable impressions of themselves (Salter 2003; Scully 1994). Of course, the desire to present oneself in a particular image is not unique to sex offenders; people in general will respond to questions and situations in a way that makes them look good (Babbie 1983). Also, given the limited number of offenders who agreed to be interviewed, the ability to generalize these data is limited. Finally, it must be recognized that the effect of gender on the research process is not entirely understood (Rubin and Rubin 1995; Scully 1994). In some instances, female interviewers are believed to have solicited more information from (male) research subjects than did their male counterparts (Rubin 1976; Scully 1994; Williams and Heikes 1993). In this study, particular attention was paid to developing a level of trust and rapport with the men. Objective questions about the defendant's conviction, probation, and employment status were asked first to help put research subjects at ease. Invasive and personal topics were discussed only after respondents appeared comfortable with the female researcher and interview process. My overall impression was that my gender and nonthreatening disposition helped facilitate open and candid discussions with respondents. Still, the gendered context here—a female researcher interviewing male subjects about crimes in which females are primarily the victims—is relatively unexplored and as such must be considered a plausible limitation.

The Sex Crimes and Their Victims

The men who agreed to be interviewed ($n = 29$) were convicted or pleaded guilty to numerous types of sex crimes, most of which were categorized as felonies. For instance, 41 percent of the interview respondents were on probation for sex offenses against children (90 percent of these victims are female). Fewer than two in ten (17 percent) of the men who agreed to be interviewed were rapists of adult women. This finding may reflect the fact that many rapists of adult women receive prison sentences, not probation. These crimes often involve intercourse, which is typically viewed as more serious than fondling or other forced/unwanted sexual actions—common among the other sex offenders supervised by this probation unit. Additionally, 17 percent of the research respondents were on community-based supervision for offenses similar to statutory rape between dating partners or friends. Although the state where these data were collected no longer has statutory rape laws per se, these men and their files describe their crimes in terms of behavior that would fall under this legal category. In other words, most of the men who were interviewed stated that their victims were "willing" partners in the sex act but that the victim's biological age (in relation to their own) prohibited legal sexual consent. Finally, nearly 25 percent of the interview participants had convictions for "hands-off" offenses such as possession of child pornography, public indecency, and Internet solicitation of a minor (all computer-related cases involved male victims). A few of the interviewees had non–sex-related convictions (usually because of plea negotiations) consistent with the actions of other convicted sex offenders but are supervised by the sex offender probation unit nonetheless because their crimes are sexual in nature even if their convictions technically were not. The most common non–sex offense conviction types (and therefore exempt from registration and community notification requirements) supervised by this probation unit are battery, unlawful restraint, and domestic battery.

Characteristics of the Interview Subsample

Table 5.1 displays demographic characteristics, offense history features, and sanctions and treatment/behavioral conditions imposed by the court for the subsample of adult male sex offenders who volunteered to be interviewed. As shown, the mean age for this smaller group of sex offenders on probation was thirty-three years old, slightly younger than the overall population of sex offenders on probation. About three-quarters of these men are white and the majority are not married. More than 85 percent of the subsample were friends or family members of their victims. In addition, more than half of these male sex offenders have completed high school or attended college (which, as indicated earlier, is unusual among convicted criminals). Most of the offenders who were interviewed did not relocate in the twelve months preceding this study. Only 18 percent of the offenders who were interviewed have previous felony convictions of any

Table 5.1

*Demographic Characteristics, Offense History, Court Sanctions, and Treatment/
Behavioral Conditions Features (n = 29)*

	% of total		% of total
Age distribution (mean=33)		No. of times relocated	
18 to 23	25.0	No moves	69.6
24 to 29	17.9	One move	17.4
30 to 35	25.0	Two or more moves	13.0
36 to 41	14.2		
42 or older	17.9	Maximum supervision	
		No	32.0
Race		Yes	68.0
White	25.0		
Non-white	75.0	Felony history	
		No prior felonies	82.1
Marital status		One or more prior	17.9
Married/cohabitating	35.7	felonies	
Not married	64.3		
		Jail time imposed	
Education level		No	69.2
Grade school	7.1	Yes	30.8
Some high school	21.5		
High school/GED	46.4	Registered as a sex	
Some college	21.4	offender	
College or graduate degree	3.6	No	23.1
		Yes	76.9
Victim-offender relationship			
Family or friend to victim	87.0	Employment (in	8.79 (.97)
Stranger to victim	13.0	months)*	
Offender's self-reported		No. of behavioral	2.71 (3.89)
prior victimization		conditions imposed	
No	57.7	by the courts*	
Yes	42.3		
		Length of probation	30.54 (3.89)
		sentence (in months)*	

Note: *Mean of valid cases; standard deviation is shown in parentheses.

kind. This finding is also unusual. Most sex offender studies are conducted on men who have serious criminal records. The demographics of
the interviewees are strikingly similar to those of the total sex offender
population that was investigated in this study.

Formal "Costs" of Sex Offenses among the Interview Subsample

The current conviction status and treatment requirements of this subsample were used as proxies of the legal consequences (deterrence and ra-

tional choice tenets) associated with their sex offense conviction. The formal "costs" of the criminal actions committed by the interviewees was two and a half years' probation (thirty months) in a highly specialized and structured sex offender supervision unit. Further, nearly eight out of ten were required to register as sex offenders. Accordingly, these men were also part of the community notification mandate, which included an online Web site where offender photographs and a brief profile are available. The percentage of interview respondents who fell under the registration and notification program is slightly higher in this subsample of offenders than among the general sex offender population studied in this research. Also, one-third of these men were ordered to serve time in jail as a condition of probation, slightly less than the proportion in the sex offender population as a whole. Finally, the majority of interviewed offenders were monitored under maximum-supervision contact standards and the average number of behavioral treatment conditions (that is, treatment conditions ordered by the sentencing court or therapist) imposed was slightly under three. Chapter 4 contains a complete list of all behavior treatment conditions imposed as part of community-based supervision within the sex offender unit.

As a review of the data shows, the demographic characteristics of the men who were interviewed were similar to that of the overall study population. This indicates that the respondents who agreed to be interviewed were representative of the larger sex offender population sentenced to community-based supervision. Still, because of the limited number of participants in this subsample, caution must be exercised in generalizing from these specific research findings.

INTERVIEW RESULTS

All respondents were questioned about their experiences with the criminal justice system and community-based supervision. In addition, respondents were asked about several topics related to their crimes. A grounded theory analysis of the data revealed the emergence of six themes. First, the respondents challenged the effectiveness of formal legal sanctions to deter sexual violence. Second, the respondents did not see themselves as real or dangerous sex offenders. Third, the respondents resented the stigma and labeling associated with their sex offender status. Fourth, the respondents reported their fear of vigilantism. Fifth, the respondents reported issues with self-esteem. Sixth, the respondents described the psychological dete-rioration (the "breaking point") caused by court-imposed requirements of community-based supervision. A theme had to appear in at least one-third of the interviews to qualify as significant. Each theme was discussed independently.

Formal Legal Sanctions

Although there were individual tales of undue hardship and injustice, most respondents attributed at least one positive outcome to their encounter with the judicial and probation system. More than one offender went so far as to say, "I would not be alive today if it was not for the help I got from the courts and my PO [probation officer]." Respondents were also asked to speculate about the impact of laws and policies designed to deter them from committing additional acts of sexual violence. A few respon-dents were reluctant to suggest that the criminal justice system's handling of sex crimes was in need of any revision. These individuals often re-sponded to inquiries into the judicial processing of sex offenses with simple answers such as "fine," "great," or "no problem." It is unclear whether the handful of subjects who responded in this fashion believed that the criminal justice system was truly flawless or if they were merely hesitant to be forthcoming about their true feelings with a relative stranger whom they could have perceived as a threat to their probation status. Neverthe-less, twenty-two of the twenty-nine subjects (75 percent) interviewed in-dicated that community notification (not to be confused with sex offender registration) is not an effective deterrent. For example, José (18), con-victed of having sex with an underage female three years his junior, states: "If you have problems, you are gonna commit sex offenses whether you are registered with community notification or not." Similarly, Bobby (49), convicted of aggravated criminal sex abuse against his fourteen-year-old niece, says: "Registration is not gonna make a difference. I don't think putting your name on a list or on a [XXX] county Web page is going to help make someone not offend or help keep the community safe." Finally, Bill (26), convicted of aggravated criminal sexual abuse of a minor female and possession of child pornography, reports: "I don't think it will deter, no, I don't. I don't think so because like, I knew about the list and being published on the Internet and all that stuff before I committed my thing [sex crime]. It didn't stop me."

These three interviewees echo the sentiments on community notifica-tion voiced by most of the respondents and documented in other research

(Meloy 2000b; Zevitz and Farkas 2000). In the absence of a comprehensive quantitative analysis on the effects of sex offender registration and community notification, the deterrent efficacy of this legislation remains unproved. It is plausible that offenders disliked the law because it, in fact, does accomplish its goal of limiting access to potential victims. Considering, however, that sex offender registration and community notification laws target the most unlikely victim-offender relationship (that is, stranger-assailant), it is doubtful that this rationale explained respondents' perspectives on the topic.

In addition to the skepticism they voiced about this policy's ability to reduce sexual violence, the majority of the respondents reported that the law is in need of revision. Their policy recommendations covered the gamut from shortening the time frame of required registration, to having *all* types of convicted offenders on a registration and community notification list, to abolishing the practice altogether. Respondents frequently noted what they perceived as injustice within the registration law: that it focuses on only one group of offenders. When offenders were probed about what they believed were the reason(s) behind the enhanced judicial attention toward sex offenders, they often alluded to its morality-based offensiveness, which, they stated, makes sex offenses seem inherently worse or more serious than other crimes. Subjects also believed that because children are frequently the victims of sex offenses (especially those covered in the media) the societal response to sex crimes is more punitive than for other violent crimes.

Given that most of the sex offenders interviewed for this research perceived a level of unfairness associated with sex offender registration and community notification laws, an analysis of their policy recommendations was somewhat surprising. For example, the most common policy suggestion by respondents was to continue the registration mandate for sex offenders (because respondents believed it served a legitimate law enforcement regulatory function) but to eliminate the public notification component of the law. For instance, Johnny (43), who negotiated two counts of aggravated criminal sexual assault down to one count of public indecency, states:

> Ah, for some kinds of offenses you should have to register. But the thing is, I, I can say, yes, you register with the police but . . . that should be it. I think that should stay right with them [the police]. Uh, with the, the jurisdiction of the police or wherever you register. . . . It shouldn't be made [public], you

know, people should not just be able to look it up. Some of the guys in group [sex offender therapy] say'n that at some [Internet] sites you can go and just pull up a picture.

In like fashion, Pat (32), convicted of sexual abuse against a minor female, says about the dissemination of registration lists:

I think registration can be okay if just the police department had that personal stuff in their files. The beauty of the police is you got 911, right? That's why we have 911. If it's an emergency you just call 911. If you think that something is wrong, something is going on, you have a question, you can pick, dial it, say you wanna ask a question. 'I know this guy by the name of Joe Doe. He lives down the street.' If you have a specific problem you can ask the police about it. They can punch it into their computer and let you know if you should be worried. But the information should not just be out there for nut cases to get hold of. This way it is used just to ask a question about somebody who lives in your community for the safety of the children and the neighborhood.

To recap, respondents stated that in their view community notification would not and could not deter sexual violence. Rather, offenders suggested policy revisions to sex offender laws that they thought would be more likely to reduce recidivism, such as registration lists that make information available to law enforcement while protecting against what they foresee as unnecessary invasions on their privacy and impediments to their successful reintegration into the community. Sexual violence scholars also express concerns about the ability of sex offender laws to deter sex crimes; in fact, many worry that these laws may prove detrimental to community safety. The overall disapproval expressed by these respondents concerning sex offender laws and social justice policies resurfaced in other interview topics as well; variations on this theme appear in a myriad of contexts in the forthcoming pages.

Stigma and Labeling

Almost without exception, respondents perceived that sex offenders are an especially stigmatized group of criminals. They referred to their social status as "deviant scumbags," "predatorlike," "monsters," and "lust-crazed animals." This theme resonated in 70 percent of the interviews and surfaced without prompting on my part. For example, Leroy, who was eighteen at the time he committed his offense, serving a term of community-based supervision for his conviction of aggravated criminal sexual abuse of a minor female, says:

> I can honestly tell you I was shocked at the level of stigma I have because of this. I mean, I knew it was bad to have sex with a teenager . . . it is obviously unacceptable and I knew I was going to jail, but ah' I had no idea I would be viewed as some kind of a child molester, predator-type thing. I got hammered by the court for this. All 'cause of the stigma of being a sex offender. . . . The stigma and how you are looked at, it's real bad by the court and everybody. It's like you're a deviant scumbag and we're gonna hammer' ya. I mean how much do they want from me? I have done my counseling, my probation, everything, fine. My therapists says I am not dangerous. They are say'n that I'm okay so why do I have to suffer and my family be stigmatized for the rest of my life? When is it over? When is enough, enough?

Gene (34), convicted of aggravated criminal sexual assault of an adult female, has similar sentiments:

> Sex offenders are treated differently, you know. I think it is because of the label that goes with being one. I mean, I have been sitting in barbershops getting my hair cut and hearing some other lady say, well yeah, "I was on the Internet and I looked up sexual offenders" and I just can't believe . . . that I am sitting in this barbershop knowing that I am this kind of person she is describing . . . a monster or something. I mean, I know who I am okay, but this label, this label that society puts on me, it's like there is nothing I can do to make it right. And this label, it is a very destructive one.

Gene and the other interview respondents appear more in touch with the stigma that they experience from being labeled as sex offenders than they are with the stigma and emotional trauma sex crime victims are left to contend with. Victim empathy (the ability to appreciate how the victim suffered and/or was harmed as a result of the offender's criminal actions) is believed crucial in reducing reoffending among these men and is therefore identified as key to most cognitive-behavior modification sex offender treatment programs in use today. Perhaps these men had not been in therapy long enough to complete these lessons.

George (21) was charged with numerous offenses at the time of his arrest, only one of which was sexually related. According to George, his attorney fought vehemently to work out a plea agreement with the state's attorney that would permit him to plead guilty to one of the felony charges (that was drug-related) and in the process avoid a conviction for a misdemeanor sex offense. George's attempt to avoid a sex offense conviction was successful. Officially, his conviction was for a felony count of possession of a controlled substance. George's case is an example of how an individual initially charged with (and ostensibly guilty of) committing a sex offense can negotiate a criminal conviction to something that is nonsexual in nature (here, a felony drug charge). Because the evidence in George's case indicated he committed an act of sexual violence, the probation department handled this case as it would that of any other sex offender. George says:

> For me, the most important thing, even more important than doing time in jail was avoiding the sex offender label. They are seen as the scum of the earth and I wanted nothing to do with that label. I don't want people seeing me that way.

In addition to highlighting the lengths that sex offenders will go to avoid the stigma associated with being a convicted sex offender (trading a misdemeanor conviction for a felony sentence), George's case illustrates how sex offender registration and community notification lists are incomplete representations of the individuals who have committed sex crimes. This reliance on part-truths contributes to the law's inability to protect citizens from becoming victims of sexual assault.

John (40), convicted of sexual abuse against an adolescent female, discusses the stigma associated with being a sex offender:

> My biggest concern about this whole court thing is that I did not want to be labeled as a sex offender. I mean, I recognize that I am a sex offender. I committed a sex offense against a minor. But, I did not want to be *publicly* [emphasis in original] labeled as a sex offender because if you watch television you see, all the time, somebody finds out they got a sex offender liv'n next to 'em and they make their life a living hell. I mean, yeah, the person may have messed up. But they either went to jail or are in counseling and stuff to better themselves. I mean, yes, they committed an offense. But there is no need to harass somebody 'cause they are labeled a sex offender. Everybody makes mistakes . . . like me. I made a mistake. Some [sex offenders] are worse than others. They want to label, they want to label sex offenders. Why don't they

label other offenders? Drunk drivers kill people everyday but they are not labeled like sex offenders are.

Devin (35) was convicted of attempted aggravated criminal sexual abuse
against an underage female. He describes how it feels to be an officially
labeled sex criminal:

> There is so much stigma I hardly know where to begin. People look at child
> sex offenders as a hideous monster kind of thing. They don't want to be near
> you. People act like they [sex offenders] are like on the verge of just, like they
> are lust-crazed animals and I don't think that is the case. I mean, don't dismiss
> them as a monster. It can be anybody. I mean, it can be your priest, it can be
> your gardener, it can be anybody, you know . . . it could be you. I never pic-
> tured myself as a monster, but going through this [court experience]. . . . When
> it first happened, I thought, what am I? I do see myself as a child molester.
> I don't see myself as the monster at all, but I see that people will view me
> that way.

Clearly, Devin, John, and the others recognized the societal stigma and
shame associated with being sex offenders but they did not think about
how the stigma associated with sexual violence impacted the lives of their
victims. This lack of insight is troubling because the ability to relate to and
empathize with the victims' emotional consequences from being sexually
violated is believed central to deterring offenders from committing additional acts of sexual violence. Accordingly, sex offenders are not successfully terminated from treatment until they master victim-empathy skills.
It is possible these men have not been enrolled in therapy long enough or
not progressed far enough to tackle these issues successfully. In any case,
clinicians and probation agents should pay particular attention to gauge
the degree of understanding and victim-empathy that offenders have toward their victims and the harm they have caused them.

Recall that the sex label was perceived as so stigmatic to these men that
one respondent accepted a guilty plea for a drug-related felony charge
(that carried a term of incarceration) rather than plead guilty to a misdemeanor sex offense conviction. For this respondent, it was more important to avoid the stigma of the sex offense label (even at the misdemeanor
level) than it was to avoid the stigma and jail time associated with his
felony conviction. As evidenced in these excerpts, respondents acknowledged some wrongdoing on their behalf, but they seldom accepted full

responsibility for the actions leading to their arrest. Subjects distanced themselves (notice the use of the word "they" and "them") when referring to sex offenders. The attempt by respondents to intellectually dissociate from other sex criminals may reflect an effort to avoid internalizing the "folk devil" label often associated with this type of violent behavior. Furthermore, the inclination to distance oneself from the category of "real" sex criminals was so prevalent that it emerged as a significant research theme independent of discussions of stigma. I turn now to this theme.

"Me versus Them"

Overwhelmingly, participants referenced how dangerous and high-risk they believed "real" sex offenders to be. Paradoxically, not a single respondent self-identified in this fashion. As such, respondents engaged in comparisons of their crimes—"me versus them"—with those of "real" sex offenders. Specifically, twenty out of twenty-nine subjects went to great lengths to differentiate their criminal actions from those of a "dangerous" or "real" offender. For instance, as Martin (51), convicted of criminal sexual assault against a teenage male, expounds:

I believe in protection against sex offenders, I think the [criminal justice] system that they got every, every neighborhood has the right to know if there is someone dangerous in the neighborhood. I would want that right too. I mean, but they shouldn't have done that with me. They put your face on the TV, you know, if I was tak'n somebody's life or doing something real serious I could see it. But personally, I just ended up touching somebody, a child, a fourteen-year-old boy. I made a mistake you know, not being in my right mind. I know I was wrong. I understand that. But I am not a dangerous kind.

Similarly, Bill (26), convicted of criminal sexual assault against an adult female, says:

Look at the consequences for rape and murder. I mean, they are real severe, you know. And they should be, you know. And well, I know I'm not that kinda person, you know, deep down you know, just, well you do things . . . out of impulse. And when you do things like that you're not thinking, snap judgment, you know. But if you're in control of your life, it don't happen that way. I'm on top of my business so that won't happen to me. That's not me.

Although this concept was not confined to any specific age group, it particularly resonated with young adult respondents. These individuals felt that court and the probation system treated everyone convicted of a sexually related offense in the same fashion regardless of the situational context surrounding the event. Without exception, participants who were eighteen and nineteen at the time they committed their crimes engaged in distancing strategies from the sex offender label. They did not believe their actions, although illegal, warranted this official designation. Rather, these subjects described their offenses merely as "consensual sex" with underage individuals. In other words, respondents recognized their behavior met the legal definition of a sex offense but they did not self-identity with this label. For example, Leroy, who was eighteen at the time of his arrest for criminal sexual assault against an underage female, says:

> They have my picture on the Internet. My friend says to me "I saw you on the Internet classified as a sex offender." Like, I got a fourth-degree sexual assault charge only for having sex with this girl. That's what I was charged with. It was consensual but she is only fifteen, going on sixteen. And I am in there with like, people like that. It makes me sick.

Similarly, José was eighteen when he was convicted of criminal sexual assault against a minor female; he reports the following:

> I am technically a sex offender you know. But I don't have mental problems like sex offenders do. I didn't mean to, I just committed an offense but I didn't mean to. It wasn't a sick kind of thing . . . But they [the court system] act like I was some sort of sex criminal.

Steve was also eighteen when he was arrested for sexually assaulting a fifteen-year-old female. He says:

> I committed just a simple offense and you would not believe everything the court did to me. Jail time and everything. I mean, it is a simple offense, as far as just having intercourse with a person. You know what I mean, I mean if I killed somebody, if I shot somebody, if I forced somebody to do something, I would feel this would all be more deserved. But this is just a wrong decision being made about me.

Steve continues this theme in his conversation about sex offender registration and community notification:

I think the list itself can be a good thing. It can be helpful in a way but like I said, not for someone like me. I should be given a chance to get off this list because I don't deserve it. I'm not that type of a dangerous person, you know.

Kevin, nineteen at the time he was convicted of attempted criminal sexual abuse of a minor four years younger than he, says:

You know what I am guilty of? I am guilty of believing the victim. I am not guilty of attempted aggravated criminal sexual abuse. For me to be guilty I would have to of known this girl was only sixteen years old and a virgin. I did not know this. I had no clue. She told me she was older. I have to register as a sex offender and I don't feel that I am a sex offender. If I was a predator or actually had or was a sexually devious person, I could understand all this. I would have no problem. But I'm not. Sex offenders should have to walk with the humiliation, that problem. If there is someone who preys on women or preys on little boys, they deserve it. But a person like myself, and I'm sure this happens all the time that somebody does not know a girl's age or a guy's age, and they have sex. And then someone comes along and says you are a sex offender. Like I said, I would have no problem with this treatment if I were a sex offender.

As these quotes demonstrate, respondents talked openly about their disapproval of "dangerous" and "real" sex criminals and identified the risk associated with these offenders as being high enough to justify much of the legal intervention to which they themselves were subjected. Still, despite the belief that as a group sex offenders pose a serious threat to society, these respondents unanimously excluded themselves when discussing dangerousness. As such, participants continually made comparisons between their personal situation and that of "real" sex offenders.

Fear of Vigilantism

Close to half (41 percent) of respondents discussed their experiences with harassment and fear of vigilantism resulting from their public status as sex criminals. Sex offenders' fears and concerns about vigilantism have been documented previously (see chapter 3) and noted in other research conducted on convicted sex offenders living within the community (Kruttschnitt et al. 2000; Meloy 2000b; Zevitz and Farkas 2000). Therefore, in part, my findings mirror existing work in this area. For example, Samuel

(33) is serving a term of community-based supervision for arranging (via an Internet chat room) to meet and have sex with a fifteen-year-old male. In reality, Samuel was not corresponding with a teenage boy but rather with an undercover law enforcement officer who represented himself in cyberspace as an adolescent male. Samuel expresses his experiences with public harassment and fears of vigilantism as follows:

> One day after I registered I got this note in the mail. It was my name, address, and my charge highlighted and downloaded off the Internet. The note said "I'm watching you." It scared the hell out of me. I mean what if somebody does something to me when I am with my kids, my family. . . . It's just not right. People will see that [registration list] and then not really know what happened because on the list it is like everybody is the same. Nobody's an individual. Like in my case, there was technically no victim. I was actually corresponding with an undercover police officer posing as a 15-year-old. You look at the list and it is as if we've all been classified as rapists.

Kevin, we recall, was nineteen when he was convicted of attempted criminal sexual abuse of a minor four years younger than himself. He shares the following sentiments about his vigilante experiences and fears:

> Oh, you would not believe what happened to me after I was released from jail. I had nowhere to live when I was released. My brother turned me down for a place to stay when I got out of jail. He says "You can't live with me, you're registered. I don't want no registered sex offender at my house. That's my family. I can't let nothing happen to them because people want to hurt you." . . . Finally, I found a place to live and my neighbors posted signs in the front yard [saying] "sex offender." I've gotten a bunch of shit happening to me because of people knowing I'm a registered sex offender.

Although the larger theme of fear of vigilante justice is consistent with earlier research, new themes related to the fear of vigilantism emerged from the data. For instance, 45 percent of the respondents who spoke of this theme in their interviews attributed their fears of vigilantism to the Internet and the easy access it facilitates for viewing the statewide and local sex offender registration list. The list contains offenders' names, addresses, and photographs and is accessible via the XXX state police Web site. Greg (23), convicted of aggravated criminal sexual abuse against a teenage female, says:

I lost my housing because of having to register. . . . My landlord has access to the Internet. She saw my picture and kicked me out because she found out I was a sex offender. I'm always afraid some nut case is going to see my picture on there, and I ain't even a sex offender, really, and come kill me or my mom.

Offenders' comments on the difficulty of obtaining and maintaining appropriate housing are troubling when placed in the context of reintegration into the community and how a successful transition reduces the risks associated with recidivism. The unanticipated consequences of the public shaming and stigma that is associated with sex offender registration and community notification should be examined to determine if there are antitherapeutic consequences with this form of sex offender legislation. It would be tragic if laws such as this one unintentionally create more sex offense victims than it spares by increasing the recidivism risk factors for sex offenders.

Bret (41), convicted of kidnapping and criminal sexual abuse of a female child, expresses similar thoughts:

Community notification can be a real problem for sex offenders. We learn about "red flags" in treatment. These are the things that can set a sex offender off and make him offend again. Well, public notification, because of the Internet stuff, people you know, they open this privacy act stuff without even thinking about its effects. Without even thinking about what it can do to a guy and his family to have his picture and everything on the Internet saying "sex offender, sex offender." I mean, who knows what could happen to a guy and his family.

Bill (26), convicted of criminal sexual assault of an adult female, says:

Registration ain't all bad, know what I'm saying. But, there are a lot of nuts out there so you got to be real careful. That's why a lot of ex-offenders don't register because they don't want people to know who they are and come kill them or burn down their house or something, know what I'm saying? And now that I got to register I am on the Internet for ten years. My picture is on the Internet for ten years. I don't want nothing bad to happen to me, but I am afraid that registering on the Internet will make something bad happen so that's why a lot of guys don't even register. They're afraid.

Many of the examples of vigilantism and shaming behavior seemed to be generated from stories the respondents heard from other sex offenders. For instance, different respondents shared similar accounts of the same story of vigilantism. This introduced the possibility that acts of vigilante justice have become a sort of folklore among this sex offender population. To illustrate, Benjamin (46) is on probation for aggravated criminal sexual abuse for molesting his teenage stepdaughter. He shares a story of vigilantism that was repeated by another respondent:

> I have heard lots of stories about things happening to guys 'cause of the registration list. There was this one man in Florida who was mistaken as a sex offender 'cause of the registration law—it wasn't him. They got the wrong guy. But he was killed cause somebody thought he was a sex offender. If a guy is so dangerous, this is just my opinion, where the community wants to burn him out and don't want him in the neighborhood, then he shouldn't be allowed on the streets. If he's not that dangerous then say so. I mean, that's the thing though. People just don't know how bad the guy is, so who knows what they might do to him?

Dwayne (22), convicted of criminal sexual abuse against a minor female, also relates a narrative of vigilante justice reported by other respondents:

> There's lots of problems with people coming after sex offenders. There was a guy, he moved into a mobile home. Then somehow they stopped the guy from staying because of the public notification, once everybody in the area found out . . . they all got together and forced him to move. Told him they would burn the house down if he didn't move.

Likewise, Alex (43), on probation for aggravated criminal sexual abuse against an adult female, reports a version of a vigilante action that was told by two additional respondents:

> This guy in our [sex offender treatment] group had fliers tossed in his yard that read "Beware a sex offender lives here." The guy's family, he had a wife and kids, were so tormented and scared by the harassment they had to move out of the house and everything.

To summarize, nearly half of the sex offenders interviewed for this research spoke of their concerns about vigilante justice and the difficulty they have securing residency because of their publicly exposed sex offender status. Offenders believed that they and their families were at risk for vigilantism and public harassment because of the stigmatic and highly visible status of being officially labeled sex criminals. Without research focusing exclusively on the issue, it is not possible to determine the ultimate public safety impact of sex offender registration and community notification for offenders or communities Many of the respondents in this group believed themselves to be more vulnerable to vigilante attacks because the registration list was now published on the XXX state police Web site, making the information available to anyone with Internet access. Data analysis revealed that the fears these respondents expressed concerning vigilantism might be grounded more in folklore than in realistic risks of harm. Although several sex offenders recounted individual incidents of public intimidation and harassment, the bulk of respondents spoke of generalized concerns of vigilante justice. Furthermore, some of the same accounts of vigilantism recurred in numerous interviews, suggesting the possibility that offenders learned of the stories elsewhere and were sharing them with one another.

Self-Esteem

Another theme that often arose in the interviews was self-esteem. Fifteen of the twenty-nine respondents (nearly 52 percent) initiated a conversation related to their self-image. For some offenders, the topic of self-esteem arose when they were asked to describe the factors they believed contributed to their own sex crime. In the example below, Tom (31) comments on how he perceives his low self-esteem played a role in his sexual abuse of a female child:

> I had real bad self-esteem issues. I mean, my view of myself was real low.
> I just couldn't seem to do noth'n right. So, when someone showed me some
> attention . . . in this case it was an underage person . . . I was too excited to
> think right. I made a bad mistake, which I don't know if it would have happened had I been in a better frame of mind.

Ricky (38), convicted of aggravated criminal sexual abuse against an underage male, reaches similar conclusions when reflecting on his own criminal behavior:

> Man, I had no support at home. Not for anything, nothing at all. So, it just
> got to the point where anybody who gave me attention made me feel good,

[and] I was going to go with them, you know just to make myself feel better about myself even if it was only on a temporary basis. But, of course, I didn't realize all this at the time. I just thought this was somebody I wanted to be with. I didn't connect the dots back to my depression and self-esteem stuff. But then, how could I feel good about anything at the time? Things were so bad for me at home so my self-esteem was nowhere.

Finally, Samuel (24), on probation for attempted criminal sexual abuse against an underage male, states:

What do I think led to my arrest? Hmm, I would have to say effects to my self-esteem. Low self-esteem can do all sorts of things . . . it hinders your quality of life for one. And it makes you desperate to feel better about the way you're feeling. You make decisions you think will make you feel better. It might for that one moment but you aren't thinking beyond that one moment. It's like, I want to feel better and this will make me feel better. You wish you had done something different now.

Accordingly, offenders believed a preexisting low self-image was at least partially responsible for their sexual violence by making them vulnerable to distorted thought processes and intense desires to feel better. However, the concept of self-esteem surfaced within the interviews in other ways as well. While some respondents linked low self-esteem to the etiology of their offending behavior, others indicated that the officially designated sex offender status itself forced them to adopt a negative self-image. Respondents in this latter category argued that their experience with the court system had affected the way they view themselves, and correspondingly their self-image. For instance, Jeremy (39), who pled guilty to one count of public indecency after initially being charged with aggravated criminal sex abuse against a minor female, says:

This whole thing [court experience] has been real hard. The money part of it is well over $50,000 at this point. I lost a lot. But I lost more than money. But what is inside that I have lost, my self-respect as a person, I may not be able to get back . . . that society has taken from me. It is deteriorating my spirit.

Darryl (34) is on community-based supervision for a conviction of sexual abuse against an adult female. When asked how his court experience has impacted him personally, Darryl says:

I don't know how to put this into words. . . . It don't make me feel good, that's for sure. It's been real, real hard on my self-esteem. And I use to have good self-esteem. It's always been important to me to dress nice. To look nice, you know. I even work on my self-esteem in my AA meetings 'cause they recognize how important a good self-esteem is. The problem is, if you ain't got self-esteem, you got nothing. And this has been real hard on my self-esteem.

Raymond (28), convicted of possession of child pornography, says:

Impact? You want to know about the impact of this? The whole thing, well, I have no self-respect left, that's for sure. I can hardly look in the mirror now, knowing how people think of me. It takes a real toll on your self-esteem.

To recap, for some offenders, low self-esteem was viewed as the catalyst to their offending behavior. These defendants described a preoffense psychological vulnerability and desire to feel better about themselves and their situations that allowed them to justify their decision to commit a sex offense. The second finding with regard to self-esteem is what offenders described as a court-imposed low self-image. This group of respondents described themselves as suffering from low self-esteem as a result of their judicial experience. Although this group did not attribute their initial criminality to a pre-existing low self-image, they spoke of a degeneration of their self-esteem brought on by their involvement in the criminal justice system as sex offenders. Without further research, however, it is not possible to determine the cause of this newfound low self-image. For instance, is this newly described self-esteem problem caused by the way criminal justice personnel responded to sex offenders? Or did self-imposed shame and embarrassment stemming from the respondent's arrest and conviction result in a low self-image? At this level of analysis, it is difficult to determine the order and relationship of self-esteem to offending behavior.

Breaking Point

The final theme that emerged from the interview data was that offenders felt they have been pushed to the "breaking point" by the justice system. Respondents indicated that the demands placed on them by the local courts and probation system were counterproductive to fostering law-abiding behavior; according to them, the requirements made it extremely difficult for offenders to complete their community-based supervision successfully. More specifically, respondents perceived that their legal obligations were so excessive that they created severe emotional and psychological distress, thereby threatening rehabilitative and community safety efforts. Similar findings have been noted in other populations of convicted sex offenders (Zevitz and Farkas 2000). To illustrate, Steve, who was eighteen at the time he was convicted of sexually assaulting an underage female, makes the following statements when referencing his court experience:

> I have people calling me a rapist now. I feel like killing myself for having to deal with this. You know, it was in the newspaper; all this stuff and I didn't even do nothing to the girl. I'm telling ya, they are driving me to the edge with all this . . . where it is gonna be the court's problem when I kill myself or kill someone else.

Likewise, Bill (26), convicted of criminal sexual assault against an adult female, conveys the following sentiments:

> You asked me to be honest so I am going to be honest with you. You can't imagine everything these people ask you to do. It is just too much. I mean, I understand about punishment to society and everything but I think all this stuff they ask of a guy might just backfire on 'em. Just for the fact it doesn't take a whole lot to go back to where you've been. It's harder to keep focused on where you're going than where you've been. And I think all this stuff they ask from you, the registration, all these appointments, all this money, the therapy, it just goes on and on. I sometimes do think it could be so much you just give up trying.

Immanuel (33) is on probation for possession of child pornography. He talked about the damaging psychological impact of the current criminal justice protocol on sex offenders:

> The court thinks they know what they doing with putting all these conditions on sex offenders. But what they don't seem to realize is what they are actually doing is creating high-risk situations for offenders and for society. Because the more stressed a person is, if he doesn't have anyone to talk to for support or a strong support group in place, and a lot of these guys ain't got that no more, he is gonna reoffend. See, that's the part that the judicial system doesn't think about. What they do to sex offenders now, I mean, I

understand the intentions behind it, but what it really does with all the reporting, the money, the PO's watching everything, the list [community notification], in many respects I think it is overkill and it has the potential to push people to that point where they reoffend. Yes, I think so. I'm afraid so.

Obviously, some respondents had strong feelings about how the local court system handled their community-based supervision. This class of offenders is monitored more closely and more frequently than other types of defendants on probation. For instance, sex offenders on probation in this locale are supervised by specially trained probation officers and surveillance agents as suggested by prior research (Berliner et al. 1995; Center for Sex Offender Management 2002; English et al. 1996; Kruttschnitt et al. 2000; Lane Council of Governments 2003). Collateral and treatment contact standards are also significantly enhanced for this group of probationers. Furthermore, local probation department records indicated, on average, that sex offenders spend more than twice as much time with their probation officer on a per visit basis than other groups of offenders on community-based supervision. Intensive long-term therapeutic intervention is ordered in almost every case. Although probationers are often ordered into treatment programs, they are usually short-term interventions (Berliner et al. 1995). In addition, three-quarters of this subsample are required to undergo STD/HIV/DNA testing and register as sex offenders for ten years.

Despite these additional court mandates, a review of the interview data and probation files revealed that only two of the ten respondents who mention the "breaking point" theme reported ever having a violation of probation filed against them. More than half of these sex offenders have been on probation for twenty months or longer, which is outside the time frame when nearly all of the sex offender recidivists associated with this research (20 of the 169 male probationers) committed a new offense. Thus, contrary to their vocalized concerns of unanticipated consequences associated with court mandates, most of these respondents were technically in compliance with their community-based supervision. This apparent paradox has at least two possible explanations. First, it is feasible that respondents have committed violations that have gone undetected by court and probation personnel. Second, it is also probable that despite their protestations that successful completion of community-based supervision is an insurmountable goal, these offenders are nonetheless performing at a satisfactory level. Either way, to understand the ultimate effects of the criminal justice response to curbing sexual violence, further research is needed: these social control measures must be examined to ensure they are not inadvertently creating high-risk situations for the community (Zevitz and Farkas 2000).

I have highlighted the six areas that emerged from the interview data. As indicated, nearly all the interviewees felt as though their court and probation experience benefited them in at least one respect and a handful of respondents credited the judicial system for providing the rehabilitation and structure they needed to live a law-abiding life. At the same time, however, the offenders interviewed for this project were quick to point out what they perceived as flaws with sex offender laws and policies. For example, 75 percent of respondents said they believed community notification is ineffective at deterring sex crimes. Other investigations and interviews with convicted sex offenders noted similar outcomes (Meloy 2000b; Zevitz and Farkas 2000). One respondent pointed to the fact that he was aware of a sex offender registry and community notification prior to the commission of his own sex offense, yet it did not deter his behavior. Others expressed similar sentiments about the inability of registration and community notification to deter a determined offender: "no list is going to stop him." Offenders spoke of the consequences of community notification (difficulty in securing housing because no one wants to live with or rent to a registered sex offender) that could potentially increase an offender's likelihood of recidivating. (Yet extant literature suggests that stable residency and employment, for instance, are both associated with meaningful reductions in sexual reoffending.)

Nearly three-quarters of respondents spoke about the stigma associated with being a formally labeled sex offender. This finding is consistent with additional empirical work conducted on sex offender probation populations (Kruttschnitt et al. 2000; Meloy 2000b). However, none of the sex offenders interviewed for this project mentioned the stigma and shame that their victims may also be experiencing. Clinicians and court personnel should pay particular attention to this issue: victim-empathy is an important factor in reducing recidivism among these types of offenders. Offenders who cannot connect with this concept are at increased risk of recidivating during community supervision.

The stigma associated with their legal status as sex offenders might explain why many defendants engaged in intellectual strategies designed to distance themselves psychologically from "real" sex criminals. The inclination for respondents to dissociate themselves semantically from "real" sex offenders was most pronounced with young adult defendants who described their crimes in terms of statutory rape between dating partners or friends. These offenders compared their "neutral" actions with that of the dangers and harm posed by "real" sex criminals. Although subjects spoke openly about the dangers posed by sex offenders, not a single respondent self-identified as a "dangerous" sex criminal. Because most of the interview participants had been on probation for nearly two years at the time of this research, it was possible that these offenders have been rehabilitated and/or deterred and are therefore no longer a risk to society. One cannot, however, be certain. Qualitative sociological research (Scully 1994), and psychological and psychiatric literature (Hanson and Bussiere 1998; Heilbrun et al. 1998; Salter 2003; Terry 2006), suggests that sex offenders often distort reality and minimize their violent behavior in an attempt to present themselves in the most favorable light.

Fear of vigilante justice was a theme that resonated with many subjects here and in other probes of sex offenders on community-based sanctions (Meloy 2000b; Zevitz and Farkas 2000). The concern seemed exacerbated by the posting of the local sex offender registration list on the XXX state police Web site. Yet results indicated that vigilante concerns of public harassment and harm may be partially based on folklore. For instance, although only a minority of respondents were ever personally subjected to vigilantism, more than 40 percent of the participants expressed serious concerns of being the target of vigilante justice. Additionally, the same tales of vigilante attacks against *other* sex offenders were shared repeatedly by different respondents and seemed to be the explanation for most of the vigilantism fears.

Self-esteem issues were a recurring theme for more than half of the respondents interviewed. For some, low self-image was seen as the root of their sexual violence. Accordingly, respondents attributed their criminal behavior to distorted thought processes associated with their vulnerable psychological state and an intense and immediate desire to feel better about themselves and their situations. For others, low self-image was perceived as a consequence of their experience with the judicial system. The specifics and order of the second relationship may be difficult to decipher. For instance, it is plausible that what respondents perceived as degrading and stigmatizing treatment by the criminal justice system actually resulted in the defendnt's low-self image. However, it is also possible that a reverse order of events was responsible for the defendant's low self-esteem. For example, Grasmick and Bursik (1990) suggest that low self-esteem can be self-induced by feelings of guilt, shame, and embarrassment associated with committing what the offender and/or society sees as morally offensive behavior.

Finally, one-third of the subjects declared that the requirements of community-based supervision for sex offenders were too extreme. Respondents felt that offenders became overwhelmed by the demands set forth by the court and as a result were rendered incapable of successfully completing probation. Respondents speculated that this court-imposed feeling of hopelessness makes offenders more likely to reoffend. And yet only 20 percent of the respondents who mentioned the "breaking point" reported ever being in violation status with their community supervision. This disjunct suggests that either defendants have committed violations unbeknownst to the probation officers or that they are somehow managing to perform within satisfactory expectations.

Respondents' perceptions that they are supervised more intensely than other groups of criminals were accurate. Probation records for this jurisdiction report the contact standards between sex offenders and probation personnel are significantly higher than for other types of offenders. Clearly, the latter two requirements are examples of court mandates not required by non–sex offender probation clients. The speculation by offenders that intensive community-based supervision may cause recidivism to increase rather than decrease is in opposition to many published studies (Berliner et al. 1995; English et al. 1996; Kruttschnitt et al. 2000; Lane Council of Governments 2003; Pettett and Weirman 1996). Nevertheless, additional research should be carried out on the unanticipated consequences of intensive community-based supervision.

To conclude, I have discussed in detail the findings from the in-depth interviews. Although the characteristics of this subsample matched that of the larger sex offender population under investigation, caution must be exercised in generalizing these data to other groups of offenders because of the limited size of the subsample. Still, these data offer a rare glimpse into the heads and minds of sexually violent men and provides a context for understanding their court experience, their criminal decision-making processes, and how these offenders rationalize their own sex offenses. There are some generalizations that can be made when comparing these interview results with those of other studies in which convicted sex offenders spoke of their perceptions concerning community notification and other criminal justice sanctions (Meloy 2000b; Zevitz and Farkas 2000).

To be more specific, the collective sex offender samples (seventy-nine men in total) primarily believed that community notification would not deter future acts of violence but that it may actually increase the odds of recidivism among offenders. "Most believed the law would have the opposite effect . . . [suggesting] the tremendous pressure placed on sex offenders by the public and the media would drive many of them back to prison" (Zevitz and Farkas 2000, 10). A comparison across studies also revealed that sex offenders in each sample felt especially stigmatized by the court process and feared vigilantes would attack them and/or their families (Meloy 2000b; Zevitz and Farkas 2000). It would be foolhardy to unilaterally disregard the perceptions these offenders have regarding the public safety impact of sex offender laws and policies, regardless of how well intentioned the laws and policies are. These findings, in conjunction with the logistic regression results covered in chapter 4, provide the basis for many of the policy recommendations set forth in chapter 6.

Conclusions and Policy Implications

We should not ask what people are likely to want to know, but
rather, ask what are the effects of community notification. If it
does not increase safety and instead promotes a false sense of
security we need to find more effective, less dangerous ways of
achieving the paramount goal of protecting children.
—Steinbock 1995, 8

I n this final chapter I review the primary purpose of this investigation
and highlight many of its findings. Even more significant, however, are
the policy implications and research suggestions that resulted from
these data and the related conversations covered within this book. I begin
by summarizing many of the factors that made this research exercise unique.
Next, I discuss the significant findings that were generated from these
data along with the policy ramifications and research questions they gen-
erate. Finally, I offer concluding remarks and my overall impressions on
how to respond to sexual violence.

As you may recall, there were several research parameters that made
this sexual violence study different from most others. For example, it
studied sex offenders on probation, something that is rarely done despite
the fact that most sex offenders will spend some, if not all, of their criminal sentence on community-based supervision (Greenfeld 1997). This sentencing pattern is continuing to grow in popularity even though little, until
now, was known about the demographics of sex offenders on probation
and the extent to which they recidivated while under the court's jurisdiction. Using probation and court records of 169 convicted male sex offenders, this study determined that most of the men on sex offender probation performed satisfactorily. Still, logistic regression results indicated that
some sex offenders are too dangerous to be placed on probation.

Next, this research augmented the typical quantitative-only analysis of sex offender recidivism with in-depth qualitative interviews conducted on convicted sex offenders. These guided conversations allowed insight into the hearts and minds of men on probation for committing sex crimes. The interviewees appeared candid and frank in what they thought about the criminal justice system and their experiences as convicted sex offenders. Victim advocates, criminal justice practitioners, and researchers can enhance community safety efforts by learning more about the motives and decision-making of sex offenders from the "experts"—the sex offenders themselves.

Finally, this project took a unique theoretical approach to studying sex crimes and sex offenders: instead of assuming that sex crimes are spontaneous and impulsive acts and that all sex offenders are mentally ill, a utility-based explanation of sexual violence was presumed. Accordingly, it was assumed that sex crimes are planned events and that sex offenders calculate potential "costs" versus "benefits" prior to engaging in sexually criminal behavior. In the end, deterrence and rational choice theories were not supported by the quantitative data. Only the "cost" side of the equation, however, was available for regression testing. There were other restrictions pertaining to the theory test as well. Given that some extant literature is supportive of the notion that sex offenders do indeed plan their sex crimes in advance (Haas and Haas 1990; Pithers 1990; Quinsey and Earls 1990; Warren, Reboussin, and Hazelwood 1998), further and more comprehensive testing is needed on these criminological tenets. The following sections contain specific outcomes from the study and the related policy and research implications.

SEX OFFENDER PROBATION

The sex offender probation unit that hosted this research endeavor began its sex offender specialization in 1996 with a declaration of "no more victims." Over the next several years they continued to shift their sex offender supervision tactics based on what experts call the "containment approach" to sex offender management (Center for Sex Offender Management 2002; English et al. 1996). The idea behind this management strategy is therapeutic intervention (cognitive-behavioral modification–oriented), combined with criminal justice oversight, close involvement between court officers and clinicians, and the use of objective testing measures (polygraph examinations) as a secondary monitoring system to ensure that offenders are complying with the rules of their community-based contracts and making accurate reports to their therapists and others about sexual actions, deviances, fixations, and so forth. The offenders in this unit were monitored more frequently and more intensively than most other types of serious offenders supervised by this probation department. They were also required to comply with specialized conditions such as mandatory STD/HIV/DNA testing, surveillance officer oversight and contact, and sex offender registration and community notification. The research findings in this study, in tandem with extant literature, suggest that a containment approach to community-based supervision is a reasonable (and potentially preferable) sanctioning option for offenders who mirror the profile of the overall sample of convicted sex offenders studied here.

SEX OFFENDERS

Convicted sex offenders tend to be older than other violent populations. The men in this investigation conformed to this pattern: their average age is thirty-four years old (compared to eighteen to twenty-four years of age, which is common among other types of criminal groups). The age discrepancy between sex offenders and other groups of serious criminals could reflect the lag time between criminal activity and detection; research reveals sexual offending begins earlier and occurs more frequently than arrest statistics indicate. About three-quarters of these sex offenders are white and the majority are not married. Nearly 80 percent of the sample are friends or family members of their victims (only about 20 percent of the victimizations involved strangers), which is similar to the victim-offender profile of other classes of violent offenses and the most common scenario for sex crimes (Bureau of Justice Statistics 2004). In addition, more than half of the male sex offenders studied here have completed high school or attended college. The level of education for this group is higher than it is for most criminal populations—perhaps explained by the fact that many types of sex crimes require deliberate victim selection (Quinsey and Earls 1990), as well as careful forethought and planning (Haas and Haas 1990; Pithers 1990; Warren, Reboussin, and Hazelwood 1998) that would not be possible for lower-functioning individuals or less-educated criminals. Thus, we have evidence as to why deterrence and rational choice theories offer promise for expanding our understanding as to why sex offenders behave as they do.

Additionally, only 16 percent of the sex offenders in this study have previous felony convictions of any kind. The absence of an extensive prior criminal record is not unusual for probation clients because the target probation population typically comprises less dangerous and "hardcore" offenders (MacKenzie and Brame 1995; MacKenzie, Browning, and Skroban 1999; Olson and Lurigio 2000). Nevertheless, this finding is unusual: most sex offender recidivism studies involve populations of men who have lengthy felony records.

FORMAL "COSTS" OF SEX OFFENSES

Part of the deterrence and rational choice model involves personal calculations of the "costs" (formal and informal sanctions) associated with being caught for a criminal act. In this study the formal "costs" started with an average probation sentence of two and a half years (thirty months) in a specialized sex offender unit. Also, seven out of ten of the sex offenders in this study were legally required to register, with local law enforcement, as convicted sex offenders and were similarly subjected to community notification.[1] Sex offender registration and community notification need to be further researched as these laws may backfire and have unanticipated consequences that could result in an increase (not decrease) in recidivistic behavior. For example, interview data reveals that many offenders believe their difficulty in securing housing or employment is a direct result of community notification. Because successful and stable attainment of these factors may be associated with reductions in risk (Avrahamian 1998; Braithwaite 1989; Hall and Proctor 1987; Small 1999; Zevitz and Farkas 2000), the impact that community notification has on public safety demands further exploration.

Roughly 40 percent of these men were ordered to serve time in jail as a condition of their probation. Given that other research has documented a positive and predictive relationship between jail time as a condition of community-based supervision and increased risk of recidivism (Meloy 2005), this sentencing option should be further explored. Despite a dramatic increase in odds of recidivism for these sex offender probationers who received a jail term as part of this probation sentence, it was not statistically meaningful and could be the result of a spurious relationship. It is possible, however, that probation is being extended to a population of sex offenders for whom it is not appropriate: that is, they are too dangerous for community-based supervision and therefore more inclined to re-offend while under the court's jurisdiction. The possibility that jail time actually makes offenders worse must also be considered. Given these possibilities, and the policy implications associated with this finding, more research must be conducted.

The overwhelming majority (80 percent) of sex offenders studied here are monitored under maximum-supervision contact standards, which mandated that they met frequently with their probation officer in the office and at their residence. They were also visited on a regular basis by the surveillance officers and required to attend specialized sex offender therapy. The officers required collateral verification (residence, employment, victim-restitution payments, and so forth) from the offenders on a weekly or bi-weekly basis and constantly monitored their treatment and probation compliance status. The frequency of contact with probation personnel and the length of contact on a per visit basis is twice what it is for probationers on general supervision caseloads. Some of the interview respondents stated that the intensity of the community-based supervision created such stressful situations for offenders that they might be more (not less) inclined to give up on their efforts to be law-conforming and slip back into their familiar criminal ways.

On average, the sex offenders were mandated to complete about three different treatment conditions successfully.[2] It was interesting to note that recidivism was positively related to increases in treatment conditions—but *not* statistically significant. Simply stated, sex offenders were more likely to reoffend with additions in treatment. Given that there was no statistical significance associated with this finding, the outcome could be the result of chance alone. Still, the direction of this relationship makes sense if you consider that more serious sex offenders are likely to be required to complete more treatment conditions; that is, they need more help or intervention to be law-conforming. Intuitively, we know that more serious offenders are also more dangerous offenders and more likely to reoffend.

Almost all of the men (90 percent) supervised in this unit were required to complete sex offender therapy successfully.[3] The role of treatment for these offenders must not be discounted: methodologically sophisticated (meta-analysis) research on the effectiveness of treatment indicates that sex offenders who complete specialized therapeutic intervention have lower recidivism than those sex offenders who do not complete treatment (Alexander 1999; Hall 1995; Hanson 2000a). Although treatment outcome research is less than perfect, there is enough evidence to recommend the continual use of cognitive-behavioral therapy as a tool to reduce sexual reoffending among probation and parole clients. In addition, prison officials and lawmakers should consider ways to fund prison-based sex offender treatment programs and encourage or mandate offender participation.

There are constraints to the positive impact that treatment can have on offenders. For example, research suggests that due to the constant and slow dissipation of benefits derived from therapy (decay process) a number of treated offenders continue to pose a risk of reoffense even after completing treatment (Hanson, Steffy, and Gauthier 1993). Because the average length of probation for this group is only two and a half years, criminal justice officials and policymakers should consider extending the length of community-based supervision in an attempt to circumvent the decay process associated with treatment and thereby reduce recidivism. Similarly, parole should be encouraged for sex offenders released from prison as it could mandate satisfactory participation in community-based sex offender treatment for untreated released inmates or be available as a way to offset the decay process of any prison-based treatment.

SEXUAL RECIDIVISM

One of the most important issues of this research is the extent to which sex offenders committed additional sex crimes while on community-based supervision. Sexual reoffending was defined as any additional illegal sexual activity that occurred during the course of the offender's probation term, whether or not it resulted in a new sex charge. In an attempt to be as comprehensive as possible, numerous sources (arrest reports, polygraph results, treatment notes, and probation records) were searched for an indication of sexual recidivism. Results indicated that 20 of the 169 sex offenders (12 percent) committed a new sex crime while on probation. This means that probation was successful 88 percent of the time or that 149 of the 169 sex offenders on probation did not appear to reoffend. On average, most of the sex offenders who failed (that is, committed a new sex crime) did so at about eight months, with nearly all of the recidivists (eighteen of the twenty) failing within sixteen months.

From a practical standpoint, this finding indicates there are time periods on probation when sex offenders are especially vulnerable to reoffending. Without additional information, I am not certain why this time frame is particularly risky. Does it take this long to implement fully the supervision of probation agents, surveillance officers, and clinicians (all of whom may be necessary to detect reoffending)? Are there especially difficult or emotionally charged issues that arise in treatment (or elsewhere) during this time frame that increase the risk of reoffending? Is the eight- to sixteen-month period simply a reflection of the time necessary for offenders to locate or identify new potential victims or crime opportunities? Is this the time span when situational (dynamic) risk factors such as housing, employment, and substance use are changing in a way that increase the odds of reoffense? Clearly, further research should be conducted to determine if this pattern repeats and, if so, what can be done to support prosocial behavior during these risky periods. Additionally, dynamic risk factors should become a more integral component of community supervision case plans and researchers should continue to assess the relationship between these issues and reoffending behavior.

Logistic regression tested the deterrent impact of formal and informal social control measures on future criminal sexual behavior and assessed what factors predicted sexual recidivism during a term of probation. Results indicate that two of the twelve variables included in the model (victim-offender relationship and an offender's prior victimization) were significantly predictive of sexual reoffending. The type of variables (offender demographics and offense history) with significant outcomes precluded any definitive findings pertaining to the impact of deterrence and rational choice models as an explanation of sexual violence. This theoretical issue should be explored further both quantitatively and qualitatively. The lack of statistical significance for most of the factors in the model is not uncommon in sex offender recidivism research because these studies are nearly always hampered by low base rates (few occurrences of the observed behavior), which impede statistically significant findings. This is one of the reasons it is critical to supplement qualitative sex offender data with quantitative findings whenever possible.

According to logistic regression results, sex offenders who were on probation for committing a sex crime against a stranger were more likely to commit a new sex crime while on probation compared to sex offenders on probation for sexually offending someone they already knew (family member, friend, or acquaintance). In fact, the odds that a stranger-assailant will reoffend sexually during a term of probation are eighteen times greater than for men who are friends, family members, or acquaintances of their victims. This finding is consistent with extant literature that shows this victim-offender relationship, although uncommon, can be indicative of a dangerous offender. As one leading clinician and victim advocate reminds us, anyone whom you don't know well—which could mean having firsthand information about his friends and family and where he works—is a stranger to you (Salter 2003). Even if you have this information, however, dangerous sex offenders are not easily identifiable. Research needs to continue to help fine tune the process. Parents and potential victims should exercise caution by staying actively involved with their children and their extracurricular activities and women should be less trusting initially of their male peers, classmates, and dates. I am *not* saying that it is up to women and/or victims to stop sexual violence but we should be mindful of where the risks lie and do our best to reduce the odds of victimization.

The other significant finding to emerge from the regression analysis is that sex offenders who reported sexual victimization in their past were more inclined to sexually recidivate during a term of probation than the sex offenders who denied any sexual victimization in their childhood. This relationship is consistent with other work that finds a statistically significant association between prior victimization of offenders and their own violent behavior (Bagley, Wood, and Young 1994; Foster, Forsyth, and Herbert 1994; Garland and Dougher 1990; Heilbrun et al. 1998; Maxfield and Spatz-Widom 1996). Certainly, one cannot claim the "cycle of abuse" or the "intergenerational transmission of violence" is a causal relationship to sex offending because most victims of sexual assault (who tend to be female) do not go on to be offenders (who tend to be male) themselves. Nor do the "cycle of abuse" theories explain why the majority of sex offenders were *not* sexually abused as children (Terry 2006). Nonetheless, because there is a significant and positive correlation between offenders' prior victimization and later sexual violence we should do what we can to break this destructive pattern. The encouraging news is that research suggests that the "cycle of abuse" can be interrupted. For instance, under certain circumstances, long-term intervention programs that ascribe to a multifaceted approach to stopping violent behavior demonstrate promising success rates at reducing further acts of violence (Spatz-Widom 1998). Therefore, issues relating to childhood victimization should be integrated into mandated treatment protocols for sex offenders. This treatment focus is often implemented for female inmates and incarcerated sex offenders; the practice should be extended to male sex offenders in community-based treatment. At a minimum, the success rate for this population of sex offender probationers suggests that further research should be conducted to establish the efficacy of community-based sanctions for similar populations of convicted sex offenders. Lawmakers and criminal justice officials should consider the potential advantages to using a community-based containment approach (Center for Sex Offender Management 2002; English et al. 1996) to sex offender management instead of relying heavily on lengthy incarceration terms that are likely to translate into sex offenders being released back into our neighborhoods without the benefit of treatment.

SEX OFFENDER INTERVIEWS

The in-depth interviews revealed six significant findings that cast light on what many of these sex offenders think about their sex crimes and themselves as sex offenders. Their assessments of the deterrence they associate with many of the sex offender policies used today were also discussed. Specifically, findings indicate that 68 percent of the men interviewed did not view themselves as "real" or "dangerous" sex offenders although they believed that, in general, sex offenders posed significant risks to the community. See what Donald (age 27) says about his Internet correspondence with a fifteen-year-old male high-school student whom he was planning to meet until the boy's parents found out and notified authorities:

> INTERVIEWER: When you agreed to meet him [the victim] did you know he was fifteen years old? Were your intentions sexual in nature?

> DONALD: Yes, I knew he was fifteen years old. Although I was interested in him sexually, I convinced myself that I was strictly going to talk to him to see if he had gone through the same things that I had when I was growing up with being gay. So I had convinced myself that I was going to just be a pal or counselor or mentor for this boy instead of a sex partner even though we were talking on the Internet about sex. I had myself convinced that I was not a danger to him and that I would never do anything to hurt someone like sex offenders do. Plus, I never touched a single person here.

As this example shows, defendants in this category took personal comfort in illustrating the differences between their actions and those of "high-risk" (*other*) sex offenders. They tended to identify their behavior as problematic, but not dangerous. One of the major goals of conventional sex offender therapy is cognitive restructuring: that is, getting offenders to recognize the harm in their actions, regardless of how the actions compares with the crimes of other sex offenders. Research suggests that as offenders accept more personal responsibility for their actions and become more empathic toward victims, they become less likely to reoffend. Therefore, it is critical that this therapeutic objective be closely monitored by clinicians and court officers.

Another significant finding to emerge from the interview data is that more than half (52 percent) of the men talked about self-esteem issues in relation to sex offending. Some of this group pointed to low-self image as the cause of their sex offending. To illustrate this point, I continue with Donald's interview:

> I got here strictly because of my low self-esteem and my secret about being gay. I was trying to live the perfect and normal life. I was married and had two kids. We had all of the material things you could want. But, in the end, it didn't matter. I was miserable as a person and felt worthless. The secret was killing my self-esteem because I grew up Catholic and was taught that it [homosexuality] was bad, so I was a bad person. How can it be bad when it's me, you know? But, still, I always felt bad about myself that I was a bad person because my church said so. When your self-esteem is that low you will do just about anything to feel good, even if it is just a temporary relief. Talking to him [the victim] gave me that relief.

Other sex offenders spoke of how low self-esteem resulted from the arrest, conviction, and subsequent consequences of getting caught up in the criminal justice system as an officially designated sex offender. Scotty (age 49), charged with sexually assaulting an eighteen-year-old female, had this to say about the impact his sex arrest and conviction had on his self-esteem:

> I have lost all my self-respect, every bit. It seems that they make sure of that in the way that they [the criminal justice system] treat you. There is no humanity left in the process. It is as if you have committed a cardinal sin and don't deserve to be treated with respect. When authority figures (or even the other inmates in jail) don't respect you, it is hard to respect yourself or have a positive self-image. I am so down on me now with all of this it is hard to know if things will ever get better.

Self-esteem issues were obviously a source of great concern for these offenders whether the issue was pointed to as a cause of the sex offense behavior or an outcome of being officially labeled, recognized, and sanctioned as a sex offender. Helping these men fully accept the consequences for their behavior while enabling them to build or rebuild self-respect is most certainly in the best interest of offenders and community safety; as such, it should continue to play a role in the therapeutic and community reintegration process.

Most of the men (70 percent) who were interviewed characterized their crimes and their legal status as especially stigmatic. "It is as if we wear a scarlet letter on our chest," one offender said. Terms such as "deviant scumbags" and "monsters" often came up in the interviews when sex offenders described how others viewed them and their criminal actions. Sadly, none of the interviewees thought of the stigma that their victims likely encountered as a result of what happened to them at the hands of these offenders. Probation agents and clinicians should monitor this issue closely as victim-empathy is believed to be critical to curbing future acts of sexual violence.

Some respondents suggest the feelings of isolation, alienation, and self-loathing that are associated with the sex offender stigma inhibits their ability to adopt a law-abiding lifestyle. Additionally, their public status as convicted sex offenders created housing and employment difficulties for registered sex offenders: landlords, relatives with housing options, and employers were either morally repulsed by the men's criminal actions or feared some sort of reprisal from other citizens for being seen as sympathetic to sex offenders. Although these positions are understandable on a personal (micro)level, they are likely to be counterproductive to achieving community (macrolevel) safety from sex offenders. Creating stressful life situations may make even relatively low-risk offenders more inclined to recidivate (Avrahamian 1998; Braithwaite 1989; Hall and Proctor 1987; Hanson, Scott, and Steffy 1995). Responsible lawmaking insists that evaluations be conducted to assess the impact these laws have on sex-offending behavior.

Public shaming has been used for centuries to punish wrongdoers and deter crime (Braithwaite 1989). However, the effectiveness of shaming and stigmatizing individuals, in the absence of successful community reintegration, has been called into question (Ahmed 2001). Research demonstrates that when shaming is used only to stigmatize and punish offenders it actually increases (not decreases) criminal subcultures and deviant behaviors (Braithwaite 1989; Hay 2001). Consequently, further research is desperately needed to investigate any unanticipated or antitherapeutic consequences associated with sex offender policies and legislation such as sex offender registration and community notification.

Another common finding in the interview data (offered by 41 percent of respondents) was the concern that community notification would result in vigilante attacks against sex offenders. The men described receiving mailed copies of their photographs and sex offender registration information that had been downloaded from the Internet with statements such as "Beware, I am watching you." They also indicated that some of the men they knew from their treatment groups had signs posted in their yard proclaiming "Danger: A sex offender lives here." Findings in this study and elsewhere suggest that sex offenders are more likely to be subjected to harassment—because of the public status of their crimes—than they are to actually be harmed. Still, it seemed a source of great stress and worry for these men; many of them stated that they lived in a constant state of fear for their well-being and for the safety of their families. Given the emotionally charged nature of sexual violence, especially crimes involving children, vigilante "justice" is a concern of offenders and law enforcement alike. One of the suggestions generated from the offender interviews was for more (not less) crime-specific information to be available on the community registries so that citizens would know that most of the sex offenders were not convicted of predatory child molestation crimes. The offenders believed this would reduce the risk that citizens would harass or harm them or their families.

The last major category in the interview data pertained to offenders' perceptions of the court mandates associated with their sex crime convictions. More specifically, nearly all the offenders believe that their court and probation experience facilitated at least one positive lifestyle change. It was not unusual for the men to state "having to come here [probation] saved my life" when talking about their involvement with the criminal justice system. However, about one-third of the respondents posited that their community-based supervision created structural barriers (in the form of excessive "costs" or sanctions associated with their sex crime convictions) that they said were impediments to their probation compliance and ability to remain arrest-free. Additional analysis, however, did not bear out the relationship between the men who spoke of "excessive" court sanctions and an increase in violations or recidivism.

With regard to the general and specific deterrent impact of community notification, 75 percent of the men who were interviewed believed that the current policy did not deter sex crimes. Many of the interviewed offenders knew about the laws prior to deciding to offend. Furthermore, the respondents did not believe it would keep other offenders from engaging in sexual violence. The interviewed sex offenders believed that registration with local law enforcement was a better tool for solving and deterring sex crimes than community notification. A comprehensive and longitudinal quantitative analysis is necessary to determine, with any degree of certainty, whether sex offender registration and community notification are effective deterrents to sexual violence. Still, it is reasonable to assume that sex offender legislation that targets the most common type of sex crime (assaults by known persons) offers the greatest formal likelihood of reducing sexual violence. Further policy recommendations geared toward increasing public safety are offered in the following section.

Many of the young adult interview respondents and their court records described their crimes as statutory rape–type offenses between friends or dating partners (that is, voluntary sexual intercourse with an underage person). As a researcher studying "sexual violence," I was surprised to learn that nearly 20 percent of the interview respondents were young adults who had sex offense convictions (and all of its associated penalties) for incidents resulting from what appeared to be consensual sex with an underage person within a few years of the offender's own biological age. In many of these cases, it was the parents or legal guardian of the minor, not the victim herself, who notified the police of the illegal sexual relationship. Although any type of sexual assault can have devastating consequences on a victim, this type of scenario does not necessarily constitute a sexually violent act in the eyes of the victim (Gavey 1999; Phillips 1999). Stated in another fashion, many women who meet the legal definition of a statutory rape "victim" may not self-identify with this label or agree that she was emotionally or physically harmed in any way (Gavey 1999). Nonetheless, these cases are often sanctioned similarly to other types of sex crimes. If the contemporary moral panic driving much of the criminal justice response to sex crimes disables the court and probation system from exercising reasonable discretion between variations in sex crime seriousness, scarce resources may be unnecessarily absorbed by low-risk offenders resulting in fewer programs and personnel to attend to more serious offenders.

The topic of computers and Internet technology were often discussed in the interviews because there were many instances when they were directly involved in the offender's arrest. The connection between computers and sex crimes has been noted elsewhere. For instance, the intentional solicitation of minors for sexual purposes via Internet chat rooms and the possession and distribution of child pornography has increased systematically as Internet access has become even more commonplace (Terry 2006). This technology has allowed more offending opportunities for sex criminals and simultaneously has made adequate community-based supervision of sex offenders all the more difficult. Probation and parole agents for this criminal population are now faced with the constant challenge of ensuring that their clients are not actively soliciting minors or potential victims online or obtaining or exchanging illegal pornographic material. Research generated from the interview portion of this study, however, indicates that the relationship between computers and sex crimes may be even more complex and involved than previously thought.

Computers and the Internet may not only introduce more offending opportunities for sex criminals; they may actually create new classes of sex criminals altogether. For instance, there were a handful of interview respondents who self-identified as gay or bisexual males and attributed their arrest and sex offense conviction to contemporary overpolicing of homosexual activity. In more specific terms, these men described incidents in which their electronic correspondence (in Internet chat rooms designated for males meeting males) was prompted by internalized homophobia among police organizations. Yet, according to respondents, their arrests were presented to the public and the court system as a legitimate law enforcement function directed at stopping sexual violence. It is unclear whether these sting operations were motivated by homophobia or just another example of criminal justice net widening—propelled, in part, by the general moral panic over sex offenders.[4] What is certain, however, is that all the interview respondents who were convicted of this class of offense had victims of their same gender.

SEX OFFENDER LAWS

In addition to collecting and analyzing data, I offer in this study a contextualized summary of how the law reacts to sexual violence. Historically, the societal and judicial response to sex crimes has been ignited by fears of stranger-assaults against children—even though such assault is a statistical anomaly (Bureau of Justice Statistics 2004). Accordingly, some sociologists argue that we are in the midst of a moral panic over the possibility that strangers will sexually molest our children (Jenkins 1998). A moral panic involves the process of claims making and construction of a social problem (here, child molestation committed by strangers) that is not supported by empirical facts (Jenkins 2001; Goode and Ben-Yehuda 1994; Best 1990; Cohen 1972). According to Cohen (1972, 9), a moral panic is created when

> a condition, episode, person or group of persons emerges to become defined as a threat to societal values and interests; its nature is presented in a stylized and stereotypical fashion by the mass media; the moral barricades are manned by editors, bishops, politicans, and other right-thinking people; socially accredited experts pronouce their diagnosis and solutions; ways of coping are evolved or . . . resorted to; the condition then disappears, submerges or deteriorates and becomes more visible. Sometimes the subject of the panic is quite novel and at other times it is something which has been in existence long enough but suddenly appears in the limelight. Sometimes the panic passes over and is forgotten, except in folklore and collective memory; at other times it has more serious and long-lasting repurcussions and might produce such changes as those in legal and social policy.

In other words, an official reaction and public concern about a phenomenon fueled by a moral panic does not reflect its real and immediate risk to society.

Sex offender registration, community notification, and involuntary civil commitment arose out of the moral panic over stranger-attacks against children. Experts agree that this policy agenda has little hope of being successful at protecting children or society at large because it fails to target the offenders who present the greatest risk (Avrahamian 1998; Greenfeld 1997; Steinbock 1995). Recall that one of the most consistent findings in the extant sexual violence literature (and in this study as well) is that sex offenders almost *always* know their victims in advance of the crime—yet community notification laws are designed to protect potential child victims from strangers, not family members and friends. Similarly, the sex offenders interviewed for this project believe that in their current form, registration requirements and community notification are unlikely to exert a deterrent effect on additional acts of sexual violence. As one offender said "registration is not gonna make a difference. I don't think putting your name on a list or on a [XXX] county Web page is going to help make someone not offend or help keep the community safe."

The available literature to date suggests that community notification laws amount to little more than a symbolic gesture in the fight to end violence committed against women and children, in part, because they do not target the most at-risk situations or offenders. Consequently, rather than settling for "quick fix" social policy measures that hold little hope for success, sincere efforts to stop sex crimes should be dictated by hard data concerning the incidents, risks, and victim-offender profile of sexual violence.

Sexual assaults between known persons are not only the most common victim-offender relationships associated with sex crimes, they can also be more psychologically damaging to victims than attacks by strangers. Therefore, social policy targeting these familial and acquaintance situations is likely to be more beneficial to victims than current sex offender laws that focus almost exclusively on stranger-assailants of children. A widespread public awareness campaign to educate citizens about the realities of sex crimes will likely do more to prevent future sexual violence than punitive measures targeting offenders (such as Florida's new mandatory twenty-five-year prison sentence for child molesters). The media should be part of this campaign to further the dissemination of accurate information. In addition to victim-offender details, this educational platform should also include facts about where sexual assaults are most likely to happen: in personal residences, automobiles, and other private locations, not in open spaces and dark alleys as many women fear. Potential victims (nearly always female) should not bear the responsibility of stopping sex offenders. Rather, potential offenders (nearly always male) should claim sexual violence as their problem to solve and undertake reasonable measures to teach young men to respect themselves and the women and children in their lives enough to avoid becoming the next offender or creating the next victim. Obviously, rapists of adult women, situational child molesters, pedophiles, and hands-off sex offenders all have unique issues so intervention and deterrence strategies will be different for these populations.

Furthermore, registered sex offenders can hardly be considered an exhaustive list of convicted sex offenders if many eligible defendants are able to avoid registration requirements due to plea negotiations (Avrahamian 1998; Freeman-Longo 1996; Terry 2006). Many of the offenders included in this analysis avoided specific sex offense convictions that carry a registration mandate because of "successful" plea agreements with the district attorney's office. We saw examples of this in these data. The process of plea bargaining between district attorneys and defendants to a less serious criminal charge or a reduced criminal sentence in order to guarantee a conviction and rapid processing of cases has become an institutionalized component of the criminal courts (Gerber 1998; Nasheri 1998). However, if lawmakers and criminal justice personnel present sex offender registration lists as a comprehensive accounting of all local convicted sex offenders, administrative and judicial reforms are necessary to curtail registration loopholes provided by plea negotiations.

The AMBER alert system is another type of legislation that is targeted, in part, at sex offenders who abduct children. The media system is designed to transmit news about kidnapped children quickly by publicizing the information over the radio and television and by posting notices on expressways. The federal government passed a national version of the law in 2003 that requires all states to participate in the notification and recovery process. The federal version of the law includes an "add on" penalty allowing federal judges to punish convicted sex offenders more harshly than other kidnappers by requiring lifetime prison sentences for sex offenders with previous convictions. Newspaper headlines are quick to point to success stories of AMBER alerts that result in recovered children. But it is still too early to know whether this policy offers real or improved protection for missing children; more research is needed.

Involuntary civil commitment of sex offenders was also born out of the contemporary moral panic surrounding stranger-danger attacks against children by sex offenders (Friedland 1999). This civil legal procedure allows a sex offender to be confined after the completion of his criminal sentence if he is deemed "mentally abnormal" and to pose a continuing risk to society. The literature review suggests involuntary civil commitment of sex offenders is excessively expensive and unlikely to make much of an impact on rates of sexual violence (Friedland 1999; Lieb et al. 1998). Furthermore, studies suggest that institutional and procedural reforms are necessary to guide criminal charging decisions and plea negotiations by the district attorney's office to respond more appropriately to the crimes of serious (and chronic) sex offenders (Friedland 1999). To illustrate, the high-profile child murder and sexual molestation cases that led to the creation of contemporary sex offender laws are examples of chronic sex offenders being released from prison early because of inappropriate offense charging and/or lenient plea negotiations (Friedland 1999; Lieb et al. 1998). Had the criminal justice system worked properly, these offenders would have been unable to commit their new crimes because they still would have been incarcerated. A social policy response to high-risk offenders that encourages and systemically supports appropriate criminal justice processing of sex offense cases is likely to be less costly and more effective at reducing sexual violence than preventive detention (Dorsett 1998; Friedland 1999; Terry 2006).

This research originated from a larger intellectual and personal interest in understanding and combating violence committed against women and children, the two most common groups of sexual assault victims. Overall, these quantitative and qualitative research findings provide preliminary support for the efficacy of community-based sanctions for many sex offenders. They also encourage the continual use of the containment approach to sex offender management and the requirement of successful performance in cognitive-behavioral modification treatment programs to curb future sex offending. The data and summaries generated here, along with the extant literature, suggest that many well-intentioned sex offender policies such as community notification and involuntary commitment of sex offenders should be more thoroughly evaluated to determine their impact on communities and victims. The greatest promise for reductions in sexual assault are likely to be associated with education programs and laws that target the most at-risk situations and offenders. Punitive and retributive responses to sex offenders are understandable given the devastation caused by their crimes. We should not let our lust for revenge, however, overshadow the ultimate goal of creating a safer world for women and children. Such a goal requires that lawmakers, researchers, and criminal justice officials remain vigilant in their desire to create policies and practices that offer realistic probabilities of reducing sexual violence in our culture.

APPENDIXES

Appendix A

Coding of Independent Variables Included in the Logistic Regression Model

Age   Measured in number of years

Race   0 = White
                                   1 = Non-White

Education   Measured in number of years completed

Marital Status   0 = Single
                                   1 = Married/cohabitating

Children   0 = No children
                                   1 = One or more children

Employment Stability   0 = 0 to 5 months employment
                                   1 = 6 or more months of employment

Residential Stability   0 = No moves
                                   1 = One move
                                   2 = Two or more moves

Stranger-Assailant   0 = Offender is a friend or family member
                                   1 = Offender is a stranger

Offenders' Victimization   0 = No prior victimization reported
                                   1 = Prior victimization reported

Prior Felony Record   0 = No prior felony convictions
                                   1 = One or more prior felony convictions

Jail Sentence

0 = Probation only

1 = Jail imposed as condition of probation

Sexual Recidivism

0 = No indication of new sex crime

1 = New sex crime during probation

Mandated Treatment

Measured in number of treatment conditions

Appendix B

Guide for Qualitative Interview

1. What crime were you convicted of?

2. How long have you been on probation?

3. What is your current probation status? If you are not in compliance, explain in your own words the reason(s) why?

4. Have the courts and probation system helped or hurt you? Explain.

5. What part of your court and probation experience do you find the most helpful? Why?

6. What part of your court and probation experience do you find the least helpful? Why?

7. Are you required to register with your local law enforcement agency as a "sex offender"? If yes, how do you feel about this?

8. How has (if at all) mandatory sex offender registration/community notification impacted you personally?

9. How has (if at all) current community contact standards with probation agents and surveillance officers impacted you personally?

10. Do you believe sex offender registration and community notification provides a degree of safety for the community? Explain.

11. Do you believe sex offender registration and community notification makes communities more or less safe than if they did not have it? Explain.

12. What circumstances do you believe caused your own sexual violence?

13. Explain if (and how) your experience with the police, courts, and probation system (for this crime) will affect what you do in the future.

14. What, if anything, can be done to reduce the amount of sexual victimization in your community?

15. What areas or things do you think researchers should be looking at in terms of sexual violence, deterrence, and the criminal justice system?

16. Are there questions that I did not ask that you think I should have? What are they?

17. Is there anything else you would like to talk about or share with me about what this experience has been like for you?

Notes

Chapter 1. Sex Offenders and Their Crimes

1. Copley News Source, "Mother of kidnapped, slain girl call him a 'monster,'" January 4, 2003.
2. NIBRS data are not available for all states. Currently, police departments representing only 17 percent of the nation's population participate in the NIBRS reporting system.
3. Given that known sex offenders are overwhelming male and that sexual assault victims are believed to be overwhelmingly female, the male pronoun is used to refer to offenders and the female pronoun is used when referencing victims of sexual assault.
4. Records did not provide any physical attributes or further descriptors of this victim.
5. Sarah Lunde's case did not fit the stranger-assailant pattern that is most typical of high-profile sexual victimization cases in that the victim's mother had previously dated the alleged assailant. Perhaps this case only garnered wide spread media interest because it was on the heels of the intensely covered murder and sexual assault of Jessica Lunsford.
6. Sex offender recidivism outcomes are most accurate when the population under investigation is disaggregated by sex offender type (rapists versus intra- or extrafamilial child molesters, and so forth): different sex offender typologies have dramatically different recidivism rates and respond to treatment interventions with varying degrees of success. Therefore, making assertions about sex offenders as a homogenous group, as is done here, will inevitably mask the failures of some groups (rapists or pedophiles) and the successes of others (incest offenders and situational child molesters).
7. There is no way to be certain what percentage of sex offender inmates actually received sex offender treatment during their incarceration.
8. Nearly all sex offenders sent to prison will be released. The only way to ensure that convicted sex offenders will not recidivate is to ban their release from prison or execute them. Moral, ethical, fiscal, and legal issues that extend beyond the scope of this book make such a proposal improbable and, most likely, inappropriate.

9. A portion of the offenders in this study had non–sex-related convictions due to plea negotiations to less serious charges (like battery or domestic battery) even though they committed sex crimes.

10. Studies show that individuals with prior criminal events are less likely to perceive a criminal sanction as certain or severe because they have avoided apprehension and punishment in the past (Paternoster et al. 1983; Saltzman et al. 1982). Stated simply, individuals with self-reported criminal histories have a lower perception of risk because historically they have "gotten away with it."

11. Although rational choice theory first appeared on the criminology landscape in the 1980s, it is not a new theoretical idea. Rather, it is part of the expected utility principle in economic theory (Ehrlich, 1973).

12. Rational choice frameworks have been more comprehensive in their inclusion of formal and informal costs and benefits associated with offending behavior than earlier deterrence research. However, relevant factors such as the role of emotional arousal on criminal decision-making behavior continue to be ignored (Loewenstein, Nagin, and Paternoster 1997). This omission may be of particular importance when conducting deterrence/rational choice research on a population of sex offenders. Despite its potential importance, the role of emotional arousal was not investigated in this present study because of ethical concerns and restrictions on conducting this type of research on a population of convicted sex offenders who are residing in the community.

13. Deterrence and rational choice (using immediate—not lagged—perceptions of costs and benefits associated with offending) were tested by having willing offenders read a sex crime scenario and answer a series of questions pertaining to (1) their perceptions of the certainty and severity of legal and extralegal sanctions; (2) their moral beliefs regarding sexual violence; (3) their thoughts on the potential pleasures of sex offending; (4) the influence of situational constraints specific to the event; and (5) their likelihood to engage in future sexual violence. However, as mentioned previously, these data have been excluded from conversation because only one respondent indicated he would be willing to engage in another sex crime. This lack of variability in the dependent variable precluded predictive analysis.

Chapter 2. Studying Sexual Violence

1. Accuracy in assessing recidivism rates among sex offenders is compromised by short-term follow-up studies: longitudinal studies indicate some sex offender subsamples experience their greatest risk period between years five through ten after arrest, while other groups of offenders appear to be at risk for sexually reoffending throughout their lifetimes (Hanson, Steffy, and Gautier 1993). Generally, the longer the follow-up period, the higher the recidivism rates for sex offenders.

Given the underreporting problems, researchers should cast a wide net (utilizing a myriad of sources when possible) in trying to capture the most complete picture of reoffending. For example, Marques et al. (1994) discovered that including community supervision files along with computerized record checks identified a 33 percent increase in the amount of recidivism that would not have surfaced had investigators relied only on national and local computerized record checks. Also, the use of polygraph examinations to augment sex offenders' self-report data of prior undisclosed sex offense activity dramatically increases the number of victims and incidents of sex abuse per offender (Salter 2003).

2. The base rate for something describes the rate at which it occurs. The rarer the event, the more difficult it is to learn new things about it. Additionally, if this rate is low (as is often the case with official recidivism rates among sex offenders) it is difficult to improve predictions (over chance) of when an event will occur. Using the typical 3 percent sexual recidivism rate for incest offenders, if we state that no incest offenders would be rearrested for a new sex crime we would be correct 97 percent of the time, even without any additional information. These factors complicate statistical efforts to improve the ability to predict which sex offenders will recidivate sexually and which will not. Finally, low base rate events often require lengthy follow-up periods to accumulate enough observations for any meaningful statistical analysis.

3. There is some concern regarding disaggregating groups of sex offenders when investigating recidivism because the degree of specialization among offenders is questionable. Sex offenders do not exclusively offend against one gender or age group.

4. Pedophiles have a sexual fixation on children. According to the American Psychiatric Association diagnostic and statistical manual (fourth edition, revised) or DSM-IV-TR, pedophiles have intense, sexually arousing fantasies, urges, or sexual activity with a child thirteen-years of age or younger. These factors must be in place for at least six months. The fantasies, sexual urges, or behaviors result in significant distress or interpersonal pain or suffering (American Psychiatric Association 2000). The adult must be at least sixteen years old and a minimum of five years older than the child victim or victims. Pedophilia is not to be confused with someone in late adolescence who is having an ongoing sexual relationship with a twelve- or thirteen-year-old (straight or gay). Individuals with pedophilia generally report an attraction to children of a particular age range.

5. Family sessions for sex offenders were usually reserved for sex offenders who were being treated in a community-based setting; these sessions prioritized "family integrity." The treatment techniques involved the augmentation of individual and group sessions along with numerous types of self-help groups (Barnes et al. 1994).

6. For a more comprehensive discussion of this topic, see the Association for the Treatment of Sexual Abusers (ATSA) at http://www.atsa.com.

Chapter 3. Legal Warfare: Sex Offender Legislation

1. The constitutionality of involuntary civil commitment is a matter of language and purpose. If preventive detention is seen as a civil measure concerned with rehabilitation and community protection, it is deemed constitutional. In a criminal context where the goals are described in terms of retribution and punishment, the law would likely be seen as unconstitutional on one or more grounds (Friedland 1999).

2. These laws were not only examples of America's commitment to rehabilitation but were also experiments in expanding the police power of the state to deprive an individual of his/her liberty in the absence of due process and other constitutional protections afforded under criminal law (Moreno 1997).

3. Most studies indicate that the rape reform efforts have resulted in only modest success for victims. As mentioned in earlier chapters, most victims of sex crimes still do not report their victimizations to police and the prosecution and conviction rates for rapists have not experienced so pronounced an increase as supporters had hoped. In practice, rape shield laws—which were designed to protect victims from harsh questioning from authorities on matters beyond the scope of the instant crime (for instance, the victim's sexual history)—offer only cursory safeguards (Bachman and Paternoster 1993; Wells and Motley 2001).

4. A moral panic involves the process of claims making and construction of a social problem (e.g., child molestation committed by strangers) that is not supported by empirical facts (Goode and Ben-Yehuda 1994; Best 1990; Cohen 1972).

5. The state of California was the first to enact a sex offender registration law in 1944. By 1951, Arizona passed a similar mandate that required the registration of convicted sex offenders. During the decade 1957–1967, four other states enacted registration laws: Florida, Nevada, Ohio, and Alabama. All fifty states now have some form of sex offender registration/community notification law.

6. In May 1996, Congress passed its first version of a federal sex offender registration and notification act. This act mandated that states must have some form of a sex offender registry in place at the local level or risk losing federal anticrime fighting dollars. In October of the same year Congress supplemented its earlier registration statute by enacting the Pam Lyncher Sex Offender Tracking and Identification Act, which provided for notification by state officials and the FBI.

7. Additionally, even in states that no longer prosecute sodomy cases, such as California and New Jersey, the retroactive component of registration laws, up until now, dictated that individuals convicted under the sodomy law of days past be required to register as sex offenders under today's statutes (Small 1999).

8. As cited in the *New Jersey Star Ledger*, December 10, 1998.

9. The National Center for Missing and Exploited Children suggests the following three criteria be met prior to enacting an AMBER alert: (1) law enforcement has confirmed a child is abducted; (2) law enforcement believes the circumstances surrounding the abduction indicate that the child is in a life-threatening situation; and (3) there are enough descriptive data available about the child, the suspect, and the getaway vehicle to believe an immediate broadcast alert will help recover the child. The New Jersey State Police's criteria for an AMBER alert states (1) that the child (seventeen years of age or younger) must have been abducted; (2) the child must be believed to be in serious danger of injury or death; and (3) that there is sufficient information available to recognize that the alert would assist in the recovery of the child (U.S. Department of Justice 2005). After these criteria have been met, the New Jersey State Police then proceed with notifying the radio stations, news broadcastings, citizens, and local law enforcement agencies to participate in searching for the abducted children.

10. These sanctions apply only to criminals being processed in the federal court system and only to offenders convicted of sex crimes.

11. This latter provision is a spin-off of the sentencing scheme commonly known as the "Three-Strikes" laws, which call for lifetime prison terms for three-time convicted felons.

12. http://www.amberalert.gov/docs/AMBERProgress0205.pdf.

13. http://www.missingkids.com/missingkids/servlet/PageServlet?Language-Country=en_US&PageId=1446.

14. Code Amber, the Year End Report 2004. http://codeamber.org/ca_2004.html.

15. Searches of legal databases such as Lexis-Nexis on post-1992 data find the term experienced more than a threefold increase in use (Moreno 1997).

16. The U.S. Supreme Court's usual stance of granting civilly committed individuals more constitutional protection came to a halt in *Allen v Illinois* (1986). The *Allen* Court ruled that civil commitment procedures were not criminal and therefore did not fall under the purview of the Fifth Amendment, thereby beginning the erosion of due process protections applicable to these procedures. The *Allen* Court came to their noncriminal ruling by claiming that the state's intention was not punitive in nature. Another major case to impact the Hendricks Court was *Foucha v Louisiana* (1992): here the Supreme Court ruled that a defendant acquitted of charges by reason of insanity may be held in a mental hospital as long as he/she is both mentally ill and "dangerous."

17. Mental abnormality is not a recognized diagnostic term in the *DSM-IV* and is a more lenient term than mental illness. Notwithstanding, the U.S. Supreme Court allowed this wording when it affirmed the constitutionality of the *Kansas v Hendricks* involuntary civil commitment statute.

18. As cited elsewhere, several high-profile cases—the 1990 sexual assault and murder of a seven-year-old Tacoma, Washington, boy by a recently paroled sex offender; the 1994 rape and murder of young Megan Kanka in New Jersey; and the abduction and rape of Stephanie Schmidt in Kansas by a man who had recently been released from prison—were catalysts to the enactment of civil sex offender legislation.

19. During his testimony Hendricks admitted to an inability to control his sexual urges when he was under "extreme stress." The state presented evidence that earlier efforts to treat Hendricks were futile and that other attempts to deter the defendant's sexual deviance (that is, incarceration and parole) had failed.

20. The Kansas Supreme Court found that the primary function of the Sexually Violent Predator Act was to further the incarceration of a prisoner, not to provide treatment; therefore it was a violation of Hendricks's substantive due process.

21. Kansas, and most other states, modeled their Sexually Violent Predator Act after the legislation enacted in Washington State.

22. The Hendricks Court defined a "sexually violent predator" as "any person who has been convicted of, or charged with a sexually violent offense and who suffers from a mental abnormality or personality disorder which makes the person likely to engage in the predatory acts of sexual violence." Individuals do not have to suffer from a "mental illness" to be involuntarily committed as SVPs. This distinction is important: traditionally, the absence of a finding of "mental illness" would exclude individuals from involuntary commitment.

Chapter 4. Sex Offenders in Your Backyard

1. Because the population of sex offenders on community-based supervision in this locale was almost exclusively male, female offenders were not included in the analysis. Because of their numeric inferiority, the inclusion of female sex offenders would have confounded research results. Additionally, a meaningful comparison across gender lines of offenders was not possible because only a handful of women were on probation for sex crimes.

2. The sample was restricted to those defendants who had been on probation for at least six months to allow sufficient time-to-reoffend and to ensure that all the social control mechanisms imposed by the court were fully implemented before the data were collected.

3. The deterrence literature in chapter 1 discusses numerous methodological short-comings associated with testing deterrence principles on cross-sectional research designs (for example, no pre- or postcomparisons of the effects of formal or informal controls). An attempt was made to overcome these methodological pitfalls by including survey data, via hypothetical vignettes of sex crimes, to measure current perceptions of legal and extralegal sanctions more accurately and to capture better the benefits side of the cost-benefit calculation. Because of the lack of variability in the dependent variable, however (very few sex offenders admitted that they would be inclined to commit another sex crime) there was little analysis that could be performed on these data; thus it was excluded from the discussion.

4. The univariate distribution revealed high levels of skewness for the independent variable "employment." Thus, log transformation (base 10) was conducted on this measure to correct the skewness.

5. According to court and probation records and the assistant director of the agency where this research was conducted, the following is a comprehensive list of all commonly used treatment options for this population: (1) restrictions on drug/alcohol use; (2) family and marital counseling (in incest cases where the family unit is intact); (3) pharmacological intervention to control impulsivity, aggression, and sex drives and the management of hypersexuality through antidepressants; (4) psychostimulants, atypical neuroleptics, and antiandrogens are further examples of medical intervention and management; (5) cognitive behavioral therapy and victim empathy; (6) apology sessions with victims when appropriate; (7) denial intervention as a separate treatment modality; and (8) dialectical behavior therapy.

6. The predictive power of the model is estimated through a comparison of the current model against a baseline model containing no predictors. The default SPSS classification cutoff is .50—meaning that a phenomenon is believed to occur half the time. To increase the predictive power of the model used in this study, the cutoff value was changed to .12 to reflect the average sexual recidivism rate (roughly 12 percent) of a heterogeneous group of offenders (Greenberg 1998; Hanson and Bussiere 1998). Additionally, the appropriateness of this classification cutoff value is further substantiated by the analysis of this research, which indicates the average recidivism rate for this population is 12 percent.

Chapter 5. Sex Offenders Speak Out

1. Grounded theory is traditionally used as an inductive-theory building tool that allows theoretical constructs to emerge free from preexisting ideas and format (Glaser and Strauss 1967).

Chapter 6. Conclusions and Policy Implications

1. The other sex offenders on probation and supervised by this specialized unit did not have convictions that carried a mandatory sex offender registration mandate. As mentioned earlier, some of these men avoided sex offense convictions through the use of plea negotiations even though their actions constituted a sex crime.

2. For a complete listing of all the behavioral treatment condition possibilities imposed as a condition of probation, refer to the notes in chapter 4.

3. Clinicians that treated the men in this study gauged an offender's progress in treatment with the use of a level system (higher levels designated progressions in treatment), completion of workbook assignments, and acceptable performance on a polygraph examination.

4. *Net-widening* is the concept of the unintended consequences of the "net" of the criminal justice system.

Works Cited

Ahmed, E., N. Harris, J. Braithwaite, and V. Braithwaite. 2001. *Shame manage-ment through reintegration*. Cambridge: Cambridge University Press.

Alexander, M. A. 1999. Sexual offender treatment efficacy revisited. *Sexual Abuse: A Journal of Research and Treatment* 11:101–116.

American Psychiatric Association. 2000. *Diagnostic and statistical manual of mental disorders. Fourth ed., revised*. Washington, D.C.: American Psychiatric Association.

Antonowicz, D., and P. Valliant. 1992. Rapists, incest offenders, and child mo-lesters in treatment: Cognitive and social skills training. *International Journal of Offender Therapy and Comparative Criminology* 35:221–230.

Avrahamian, K. 1998. A critical perspective: Do 'Megan's Laws' really shield children from sex predators? *Journal of Juvenile Law* 19:1–18.

Babbie, E. 1983. *The practice of social research*. Belmont, Calif.: Wadsworth.

Bachman, R., and R. Paternoster. 1993. A contemporary look at the effects of rape law reform: How far have we really come? *Journal of Criminal Law and Criminology* 84:554–574.

Bachman, R., R. Paternoster, and S. Ward. 1992. The rationality of sexual offend-ing: Testing a deterrence/rational choice conception of sexual assault. *Law and Society Review* 26:343–372.

Bagley, C., M. Wood, and L. Young. 1994. Victim to abuser: Mental health and behavioral sequels of child sexual abuse in a community survey of young adult males. *Child Abuse and Neglect* 18:683–697.

Baker, W. 1984. Castration of the male offenders: A legally impermissible alter-native. *Loyola Law Review* 30:377–399.

Barbaree, H., and W. Marshall. 1988. Deviant sexual arousal, offense history, and demographic variables as predictors of re-offense among child molesters. *Be-havioral Sciences and the Law* 6:267–280.

Barnes, A., M. Baca, M. Dix, S. Flahr, C. Gaal, M. Whitaker, S. Moeglein, and N. Morgheim. 1994. *Sex offender treatment project: Literature review*. Report prepared for Alaska Department of Corrections. Anchorage: Justice Center, University of Alaska Anchorage, 1–29.

Becker, J. V. 1994. Offenders: Characteristics and treatment. *The Future of Chil-dren* 4:176–197.

Becker, J. V., and J. A. Hunter. 1992. Evaluation of treatment outcome for adult perpetrators of child sexual abuse. *Criminal Justice and Behavior* 19: 74–92.

Bedarf, A. 1995. Examining sex offender community notification laws. *California Law Review* 83:885–939.

Belknap, J. 2001. *The invisible woman: Gender, crime, and justice.* Belmont, Calif.: Wadsworth.

Bellair, P. 1997. Social interaction and community crime: Examining the importance of neighbor networks. *Criminology* 35:677–703.

Berliner, L., D. Schram, L. Miller, and C. Milloy. 1995. A sentencing alternative for sex offenders: A study of decision making and recidivism. *Journal of Interpersonal Violence* 10:487–502.

Best, J. 1990. *Threatened children: Rhetoric and concern about child-victims.* Chicago: University of Chicago Press.

Braithwaite, J. 1989. *Crime, shame, and reintegration.* Cambridge: Cambridge University Press.

Browne, K., and M. Lynch. 1995. The nature and extent of child homicide and fatal abuse. *Child Abuse Review* 4:309–316.

Bureau of Justice Statistics. 2004. *Criminal victimization, 2003.* Washington, D.C.: U.S. Department of Justice.

Center for Sex Offender Management. 2001. *Recidivism of sex offenders.* Washington, D.C.: U.S. Department of Justice.

———. 2002. *Managing sex offenders in the community: A handbook to guide policymakers and practitioners through a planning and implementation process.* Washington, D.C.: U.S. Department of Justice.

Centers for Disease Control and Prevention. 2004. Sexual assault awareness. http://www.cdc.gov/ncipc/dvp/saam.htm.

Classen, C., O. Palesh, and R. Aggarwal. 2005. Sexual revictimization: A review of the empirical literature. *Trauma, Violence, and Abuse* 6:103–129.

Cohen, S. 1972. *Folk devils and moral panics: The creation of the mods and rockers.* London: MacGibbon and Kee.

Connecticut Department of Public Safety v John Doe. 2002. http://www.supreme court.us.gov/opinions/02pdf/01–1231.pdf.

Conte, J. R., and J. R. Schuerman. 1987. Factors associated with an increased impact of child sexual abuse. *Child Abuse and Neglect* 13:201–211.

Cornish, D. B., and R. Clarke. 1986. *The reasoning criminal: Rational choice perspectives on offending.* New York: Springer-Verlag.

DeKeseredy, W., and M. Schwartz. 1998. *Woman abuse on campus: Results from the Canadian national survey.* Thousand Oaks, Calif.: Sage.

DeMatteo, D. 1998. Welcome to Anytown, USA—home of beautiful scenery (and a convicted sex offender): Sex offender registration and notification laws. *Villanova Law Review* 43:1–58.

Denzin, N. 1997. *Interpretive ethnography: Ethnographic practices for the 21st century.* Thousand Oaks, Calif.: Sage.

Dobash, E., and R. Dobash. 1979. *Violence against wives: A case against the patriarchy.* New York: Free Press.

Doe v Portiz. 1995. 662 A.2d 367 (New Jersey), 4. http://parents_united.tripod.com/Megan2.htm.

Dorsett, K. 1998. *Kansas v Hendricks:* Marking the beginning of a dangerous new era in civil commitment. *DePaul Law Review* 48:1–54.

Ehrlich, I. 1973. Participation in illegitimate activities: A theoretical and empirical investigation. *Journal of Political Economy* 81:516–521.

English, K., S. Pullen, and L. Jones. 1996. *Managing adult sex offenders: A containment approach.* Boulder, Colo.: American Probation and Parole Association.

Faravelli, C., A. Giugni, S. Salvatori, and V. Ricca. 2004. Psychopathology after rape. *American Journal of Psychiatry* 161:1483–1485.

Finkelhor, D. 1984. *Child sexual abuse: New theory and research.* New York: Free Press.

———. 1994. Current information on the scope and nature of child sexual abuse. *Child Abuse and Neglect* 4:31–53.

Finkelhor, D., and A. Lewis. 1988. An epidemiologic approach to the study of child molestation. In *Human sexual aggression: Current perspectives,* edited by R. Prentky and V. Quinsey, 64–78. New York: New York Academy of Sciences.

Finn, P. 1997. *Sex offender community notification.* Research in Action (pp. 1–19). Washington, D.C.: National Institute of Justice, U.S. Department of Justice.

Fisher, B., and J. Sloan. 2003. Unraveling the fear of victimization among college women: Is the 'shadow of sexual assault' hypothesis supported? *Justice Quarterly* 20:633–659.

Fisher, B., F. Cullen, and M. Turner. 2000. *The sexual victimization of college women.* Washington, D.C.: U.S. Department of Justice.

Fisher, D., and D. Thornton. 1993. Assessing risk of re-offending in sexual offenders. *Journal of Mental Health* 2:105–117.

Ford, D., R. Bachman, M. Friend, and M. Meloy. 2002. *Controlling violence against women: A research perspective on the 1994 VAWA's criminal justice impacts.* Washington, D.C.: National Institute of Justice, U.S. Department of Justice.

Foster, B., C. Forsyth, and S. Herbert. 1994. The cycle of family violence among criminal offenders: A study of inmates in one Louisiana jail. *Free Inquiry in Creative Sociology* 22:1–5.

Freedman, B. 1987. Equipoise and the ethics of clinical research. *New England Journal of Medicine* 317:141–145.

Freeman-Longo, R. 1996. Feel good legislation: Prevention or calamity. *Child Abuse & Neglect* 20:95–101.

Friedland, S. 1999. On treatment, punishment, and the civil commitment of sex offenders. *University of Colorado Law Review* 70:73–154.

Garland, R., and M. Dougher. 1990. The abused/abuser hypothesis of child abuse: A critical review of theory and research. In *Pedophilia: Biosocial dimensions*, edited by J. R. Feierman, 488–509. New York: Springer-Verlag.

Gavey, N. 1999. "I wasn't raped, but . . .": Revisiting definitional problems in sexual victimization. In *New versions of victims: Feminist struggles with the concept*, edited by S. Lamb, 57–81. New York: New York University Press.

Gerber, R. 1998. A judicial view of plea bargaining. *Criminal Law Bulletin* 34: 16–31.

Glaser, B., and A. Strauss. 1967. *The discovery of grounded theory: Strategies for qualitative research*. New York: Aldine.

Golding, J. 1996. Sexual assault history and limitations in physical functioning in two general populations samples. *Research Nursing Health* 19:33–44.

Goode, E. and N. Ben-Yehuda. 1994. *Moral panics: The social construction of deviance*. Cambridge, Mass.: Blackwell.

Goode, E., and B. Nachman. 1994. Moral panics: Culture, politics, and social construction. *Annual Review of Sociology* 20:149–171.

Grasmick, H., and R. Bursik, Jr. 1990. Conscience, significant others, and rational choice: Extending the deterrence model. *Law and Society Review* 24: 837–861.

Greenberg, D. 1998. Sexual recidivism in sex offenders. *Canadian Journal of Psychiatry* 43:459–465.

Greenfeld, L. A. 1997. *Sex offenses and offenders: An analysis of data on rape and sexual assault*. Washington, D.C.: U.S. Department of Justice, Bureau of Justice Statistics.

Haas, L., and J. Haas. 1990. *Understanding sexuality*. Boston: Mosby.

Hall, G. 1995. Sex offender revisited: A meta-analysis of recent treatment studies. *Journal of Consulting and Clinical Psychology* 63:802–809.

Hall, G., and W. C. Proctor. 1987. Criminological predictors of recidivism in a sexual offender population. *Journal of Consulting and Clinical Psychology* 55:111–112.

Hanson, R. K. 1998. What do we know about sex offender risk assessment? *Psychology, Public Policy and Law* 4:50–72.

———. 2000a. *The effectiveness of treatment for sexual offenders: Report to the Association for the Treatment of Sexual Abusers Collaborative Data Research Committee*. Presentation at the Association for the Treatment of Sexual Abusers' Nineteenth Annual Research and Treatment Conference, San Diego, Calif.

———. 2000b. Will they do it again? Predicting sex offender recidivism. *Current Directions in Psychological Science* 9:106–109.

Hanson, R. K., and M. Bussiere. 1998. Predicting relapse: A meta-analysis of sexual offender recidivism studies. *Journal of Counseling and Clinical Psychology* 66:348–362.

Hanson, R. K, H. Scott, and R. Steffy. 1995. A comparison of child molesters and nonsexual criminals: Risk predictors and long-term recidivism. *Journal of Research in Crime and Delinquency* 32:325–337.

Hanson, R. K, R. Steffy, and R. Gauthier. 1993. Long-term recidivism of child molesters. *Journal of Consulting Clinical Psychology* 61:646–652.

Hanson, R. K, and D. Thornton. 2000. Improving risk assessments for sex offenders: A comparison of three actuarial scales. *Law and Human Behavior* 24: 57–66.

Harris, G., M. Rice, and V. Quinsey. 1993. Violent recidivism of mentally disordered offenders: The development of a statistical prediction instrument. *Criminal Justice and Behavior* 20:315–335.

Hay, C. 2001. An exploratory test of Braithwaite's reintegrative shaming theory. *Journal of Research in Crime and Delinquency* 38:132–153.

Heilbrun, K., C. Nezu, M. Keeney, S. Chung, and A. Wasserman, A. (1998). Sexual offending: Linking assessment, intervention, and decision-making. Psychology, *Public Policy, and Law* 4:138–174.

Hepburn, J., and M. Griffin. 2004. The effect of social bonds on successful adjustment to probation: An event history analysis. *Criminal Justice Review* 29:46–75.

Janus, E. 1996. Preventing sexual violence: Setting principled constitutional boundaries on sex offender commitments. *Indiana Law Journal* 72:157–214.

———. 1997. The use of social science and medicine in sex offender commitment. *New England Journal on Criminal and Civil Confinement* 23:1–26.

———. 2003. Examining our approaches to sex offenders and the law, Minnesota's sex offender commitment program: Would an empirically-based prevention policy be more effective? *William Mitchell Law Review* 29:1–37.

Jenkins, P. 1998. *Moral panic: Changing concepts of the child molester in modern America.* New Haven, Conn.: Yale University Press.

———. 2001. *Beyond tolerance: Child pornography on the Internet.* New York: New York University Press.

Kansas v Hendricks. 1997. 117 S. Ct. 2072, 2078. http://biotech.law.lsu.edu/cases/psyc/kansas_v_hendricks.htm

Kilpatrick, D. G., C. N. Edmunds, and A. K. Seymour. 1992. *Rape in America: A report to the nation.* Arlington, Va.: National Victim Center and Medical University of South Carolina.

Klepper, S., and D. Nagin. 1989. The deterrent effect of perceived certainty and severity of punishment revisited. *Criminology* 27:721–746.

Koss, M. P., and L. Heslet. 1992. Somatic consequences of violence against women. *Archives of Family Medicine* 1:53–59.

Kruttschnitt, C., C. Uggen, and K. Shelton. 2000. Predictors of desistance among sex offenders: The interaction of formal and informal social controls. *Justice Quarterly* 17:62–87.

La Fond, J. 1998. The costs of enacting a sexual predator law. *Psychology, Public Policy and Law* 4:468–504.

————. 1999. Therapeutic jurisprudence: Can it be normatively neutral? Sexual predator laws: Their impact on participants and policy. *Arizona Law Review* 41:1–45.

La Fontaine, J. S. 1990. *Child sexual abuse.* Cambridge: Polity.

Lamb, S. 1996. *The trouble with blame: Victims, perpetrators, and responsibility.* Cambridge, Mass.: Harvard University Press.

Lane Council of Governments. 2003. *Managing sex offenders in the community: A national overview.* Washington, D.C.: U.S. Department of Justice, Office of Justice Programs.

Langan, P., and D. Levin. 2002. *Recidivism of prisoners released in 1994.* Washington, D.C.: U.S. Department of Justice.

Langan, P., E. Schmitt, and M. Durose. 2003. *Recidivism of sex offenders released from prison in 1994.* Washington, D.C: U.S. Department of Justice.

Laub, J., D. Nagin, and R. Sampson. 1998. Trajectories of change in criminal offending: Good marriages and the desistance process. *American Sociological Review* 63:225–238.

Lewis, R. 1988. *Effectiveness of statutory requirements for the registration of sex offenders: A report to the California state legislature.* N.P.: California Department of Justice.

Lieb, R., V. Quinsey, and L. Berliner. 1998. Sexual predators and social policy. *Crime and Justice* 23:2–49.

Loewenstein, G., D. Nagin, and R. Paternoster. 1997. The effect of sexual arousal on expectations of sexual forcefulness. *Journal of Research in Crime and Delinquency* 34:443–473.

Lofland, J., and L. Lofland. 1995. *Analyzing social settings: A guide to qualitative observation and analysis.* Belmont, Calif.: Wadsworth.

Lotke, E. 2005. *Issues and answers, Sex offenders: Does treatment work?* Alexandria, Va.: National Center on Institutions and Alternatives. http://66.165.94 .98/stories/sexoffend.html (accessed September 23, 2005).

Lucken, K., and J. Latina. 2002. Sex offender civil commitment laws: Medicalizing deviant sexual behavior. *Barry Law Review* 15:1–19.

MacKenzie, D. L., and R. Brame. 1995. Shock incarceration and positive adjustment during community supervision. *Journal of Quantitative Criminology* 11: 111–142

MacKenzie, D. L., K. Browning, and S. Skroban. 1999. The impact of probation on the criminal activities of offenders. *Journal of Research in Crime and Delinquency* 36:423–453.

Mailloux, D. J. Abracen, R. Serin, C. Cousineau, B. Malcolm, and J. Looman. 2003. Dosage of treatment to sexual offenders: Are we overprescribing? *International Journal of Offender Therapy and Comparative Criminology* 47:171–184.

Marge, D. 2003. *A call to action: Ending crimes of violence against children and adults with disabilities.* Syracuse, N.Y.: SUNY Upstate Medical University.

Marques, J., D. Day, C. Nelson, and M. West. 1994. Effects of cognitive-behavioral treatment on sex offender recidivism. *Criminal Justice and Behavior* 21:28–54.

Marques, J. N. 1970. Orgasmic reconditioning: Changing sexual object choice through controlling masturbation fantasies. *Journal of Behavior Therapy and Experimental Psychiatry* 1:263–271.

Marshall, W. L. 1996. Assessment, treatment, and theorizing about sex offenders: Development during the past twenty years. *Criminal Justice and Behavior* 23:162–199.

Marshall, W. L., D. Anderson, and Y. Fernandez. 1999. *Cognitive behavioural treatment of sexual offenders.* New York: John Wiley and Sons.

Marshall, W. L., and H. E. Barbarbee. 1990. An integrated theory of sexual offending. In *Handbook of sexual assaults: Issues, theories and treatment of the offender,* edited by W. L. Marshall, D. R. Laws, and H. E. Barbaree, 257–275. New York: Plenum Press.

Marshall, W. L., R. Jones, I. Ward, P. Johnston, and H. E. Barbaree. 1991. Treatment outcome with sex offenders. *Clinical Psychological Review* 2: 465–478.

Marshall, W., and W. Pithers. 1994. A reconsideration of treatment outcome with sex offenders. *Criminal Justice and Behavior* 21:10–27.

Maxfield, M., and C. Spatz-Widom. 1996. The cycle of violence: Revisited after six years. *Archives of Pediatric and Adolescent Medicine* 150:390–395.

McGrath, R., S. Hoke, and J. Vojtisek. 1998. Cognitive-behavioral treatment of sex offenders: A treatment comparison and long-term follow-up study. *Criminal Justice and Behavior* 25:203–225.

McGuire, R. J., and M. Vallance. 1964. Aversion therapy by electric shock: A simple technique. *British Medical Journal* 2:594–597.

Meadows, R. 2001. *Understanding violence and victimization.* Upper Saddle River, N.J.: Prentice Hall.

Meloy, M. 2000a. Prediction by proxy: The reliability of traditional correlates of criminal recidivism and chronic sex offending. Unpublished manuscript

———. 2000b. Stranger danger: Problems with community notification. In *Myths, risks and sexuality,* edited by K. Buckley and P. Head, 11–26. Dorset, U.K.: Russell House.

———. 2005. The sex offender next door: An analysis of recidivism, risk factors, and deterrence of sex offenders on probation. *Criminal Justice Policy Review* 16:211–236.

Meyers, M. 1997. *News coverage of violence against women: Engendering blame.* Thousand Oaks, Calif.: Sage.

Miller, S., and M. Meloy. 2000. Women on the bench: Mavericks, peace makers, or something else?: Research questions, issues and suggestions. In *It's a crime: Women and justice,* edited by R. Muraskin and T. Alleman, 53–68. Englewood Cliffs, N.J.: Regents–Prentice Hall.

————. 2006. *Exploring victim policies and politics of violence against women.* New York: Oxford University Press.

Moreno, J. 1997. Whoever fights monsters should see to it that in the process he does not become a monster. *Florida Law Review* 49:1–54.

Mossman, D. 1994. Assessing predictions of violence: Being accurate about accuracy. *Journal of Consulting and Clinical Psychology* 62:783–792.

Nagin, D., D. P. Farrington, and T. Moffitt. 1995. Life course trajectories of different types of offenders. *Criminology* 33:111–139.

Nagin, D., and R. Paternoster. 1993. Enduring individual differences and rational choice theories of crime. *Law and Society Review* 27:467–496.

Nasheri, H. 1998. *Betrayal of due process: A comparative assessment of plea bargaining in the United States and Canada.* Lanham, Md.: University Press of America.

National Center for Institutions and Alternatives. 1996. Community Notification and Setting the Record Straight on Recidivism. http://www.ncianet.org/ncia/comnot.html.

O'Grady, W., M. Asbridge, and T. Abernathy. 2000. Illegal tobacco sales to youth: A view from rational choice theory. *Canadian Journal of Criminology* 42:1–16.

Olson, D., and A. Lurigio. 2000. Predicting probation outcomes: Factors associated with probation re-arrest, revocations, and technical violations during supervision. *Justice Research and Policy* 2:73–86.

Otte v Doe. 2001. http://supreme.lp.findlaw.com/supreme_court/briefs/01–729/01–729.mer.ami.rcfp.pdf.

Paternoster, R. 1989a. Absolute and restrictive deterrence in a panel of youth: Explaining the onset, persistence/desistance, and frequency of delinquent offending. *Social Problems* 36:289–309.

————. 1989b. Decisions to participate in and desist from four types of common delinquency: Deterrence and the rational choice perspective. *Law and Society Review* 23:7–40.

Paternoster, R., L. Saltzman, G. Waldo, and T. Chircos. 1983. Perceived risks and social control: Do sanctions really deter? *Law and Society Review* 17:457–480.

PBSJ. 2004. *Amber, emergency, and travel time messaging guidance for transportation agencies.* Final report prepared for U.S. Department of Transportation. Columbus, Ohio. 1–22.

Petersilia, J., and S. Turner. 1993. Intensive probation and parole. *Crime and Justice: A Review of Research* 17, edited by M. Tonry, 281–336. Chicago: University of Chicago Press.

Pettett, J., and D. Weirman. 1996. Monitoring with surveillance officers. In *Managing adult sex offenders: A containment approach,* edited by K. English, S. Pullen, and L. Jones, 11.1–11.11. Boulder, Colo.: American Probation and Parole Association.

Phillips, L. 1999. Recasting consent: Agency and victimization in adult-teen relationships. In *New versions of victims: Feminists struggle with concept,* edited by S. Lamb, 82–107. New York: New York University Press.

Piliavin, I., R. Gartner, C. Thornton, and R. Matsueda. 1986. Crime deterrence and rational choice. *American Sociological Review* 51:101–119.

Piquero, A., and S. Tibbetts. 1996. Specifying the direct and indirect effects of low self-control and situational factors in offenders' decision making: Toward a more complete model of rational offending. *Justice Quarterly* 13:481–508.

Pithers, W. 1990. Relapse prevention with sexual aggression: A method for maintaining therapeutic gain and enhancing external supervision. In *Handbook of sexual assault: Issues, theories, and treatment of the offender,* edited by W. L. Marshall, D. R. Laws, and H. E. Barbaree, 343–361. New York: Plenum.

Pleck, E. 1987. *Domestic tyranny.* New York: Oxford University Press.

Pratt, J. 1998. The rise and fall of homophobia and sexual psychopath legislation in postwar society. *Psychology, Public Policy, and Law* 1:25–49.

Prentky, R., R. Knight, and A. Lee. 1997. Risk factors associated with recidivism among extrafamilial child molesters. *Journal of Consulting and Clinical Psychology* 65:141–149.

Prentky, R., A. Lee, R. Knight, and D. Cerce. 1997. Recidivism rates among child molesters and rapists: A methodological analysis. *Law and Human Behavior* 21:635–658.

Pritchard, C., and C. Bagley. 2001. Suicide and murder in child murderers and child sexual abusers. *Journal of Forensic Psychiatry* 12:269–286.

Quinsey, V., and C. Earls. 1990. The modification of sexual preferences. In *Handbook of sexual assault: Issues, theories, and treatment of the offender* edited by W. L. Marshall, D. R. Laws, and H. E. Barbaree, 279–295. New York: Plenum.

Quinsey, V., M. Rice, and G. Harris. 1995. Actuarial prediction of sexual recidivism. *Journal of Interpersonal Violence* 10:85–105.

Rice, M. 1997. Violent offender research and implications for the criminal justice system. *American Psychologist* 52:414–423.

Rice, M., and G. Harris. 1997. Cross-validation and extension of the violence risk appraisal guide for child-molesters and rapists. *Law and Human Behavior* 21:231–241.

Rice, M., V. Quinsey, and G. Harris. 1991. Sexual recidivism among child molesters released from maximum security psychiatric institution. *Journal of Consulting Clinical Psychology* 59:381–386.

Rubin, H., and I. Rubin. 1995. *Qualitative interviewing: The art of hearing data.* London: Sage.

Rubin, L. 1976. *Worlds of pain.* New York: Basic Books.

Salter, A. 1995. *Transforming trauma: A guide to understanding and treating adult survivors of child sexual abuse.* Thousand Oaks, Calif.: Sage.

————. 2003. *Predators: Pedophiles, rapists and other sex offenders.* New York: Basic Books.

Saltzman, L., R. Paternoster, G. Waldo, and T. Chiricos. 1982. Deterrent and experiential effects: The problem of causal order in perceptual deterrence research. *Journal of Research in Crime and Delinquency* 19:172–189.

Sapp, A., and M. Vaughn. 1991. Sex offender rehabilitation programs in state prisons: A nationwide survey. *Journal of Offender Rehabilitation* 17:55–75.

Schram, D., and C. Milloy. 1995. *Community notification: A study of offender characteristics and recidivism.* Washington State Institute for Public Policy. Seattle, Wash.: Urban Policy Research.

Scully, D. 1994. *Understanding sexual violence: A study of convicted rapists.* New York: Routledge.

Shover, N., and C. Thompson. 1992. Age, differential expectations, and crime desistance. *Criminology* 30:89–104.

Skinner, B. F. 1953. *Science and human behavior.* New York: Macmillian.

Small, J. 1999. Who are the people in your neighborhood? Due process, public protection, and sex offender notification laws. *New York University Law Review* 74:1465–1467.

Snyder, H. 2000. *Sexual assault of young children as reported to law enforcement: Victim, incident, and offender characteristics.* Washington, D.C: Bureau of Justice Statistics, U.S. Department of Justice.

Spohn, C., and J. Horney. 1992. *Rape law reform: A grassroots revolution and its impact.* New York: Plenum.

Spatz-Widom. 1998. Child victims: Searching for opportunities to break the cycle of violence. *Applied and Preventive Sociology* 7:225–234.

Steinbock, B. 1995. A policy perspective. (New Jersey), Megan's Law: Community notification of the release of sex offenders. *Criminal Justice Ethics* 14:4–9.

Strauss, A., and J. Corbin. 1998. *Basics of qualitative research.* London: Sage.

Terry, K. 2006. *Sexual offenses and offenders: Theory, practice, and policy.* Belmont, Calif.: Wadsworth.

Tjaden, P., and N. Thoennes. 2000. *Full report of the prevalence, incidence, and consequences of violence against women: Findings from the national violence against women survey.* Washington, D.C.: National Institute of Justice and the Centers for Disease Control and Prevention.

Turner, B., J. Bingham, and F. Andrasik. 2000. Short-term community-based treatment for sexual offenders: Enhancing effectiveness. *Sexual Addiction & Compulsivity* 7:211–223.

Turner, S., J. Petersilia, and E. Deschenes. 1992. Evaluating intensive supervision probation/parole for drug offenders. *Crime and Delinquency* 38:539–556.

Ullman, S. 2004. Sexual assault victimization and suicidal behavior in women: A review of the literature. *Aggression and Violent Behavior* 9:331–351.

United States v Salerno. 1987. 481 U.S. 739, 747. http://www.thelaborers.net/court_cases/us_v_salerno_no_86–87.htm

U.S. Department of Health and Human Services, Administration on Children, Youth, and Families. 2005. *Child Maltreatment 2003.* Washington, D.C.: U.S. Government Printing Office.

U.S. Department of Justice. 2005. *Progress Report on the National AMBER Alert Strategy.* Office of Justice Programs.

Warren, J., R. Reboussin, and R. Hazelwood. 1998. Crime scene and distance correlates of serial rape. *Journal of Quantitative Criminology* 14:35–39.

Wells, C., and E. Motley. 2001. Reinforcing the myth of the crazed rapist: A feminist critique of recent rape legislation. *Boston University Law Review* 81:1–60.

Williams, C., and J. Heikes. 1993. The importance of researcher's gender in the in-depth interview: Evidence from two case studies of male nurses. *Gender and Society* 7:280–291.

Williams, K., and R. Hawkins. 1986. Perceptual research on general deterrence: A critical review. *Law and Society Review* 20:545–572.

Zevitz, R. 2004. Sex offender placement and neighborhood social integration: The making of a scarlet letter community. *Criminal Justice Studies* 17:203–222.

Zevitz, R., and M. Farkas. 2000. *Sex offender community notification: Assessing the impact in Wisconsin.* Research in Action. Washington, D.C.: U.S. Department of Justice.

Index

AMBER alerts: definition of, 6, 44–45, 127n.9, 127n.12, 127n.14; effectiveness of, 45–47; examples of successes, 46, 114; federal version of, 45; improper use of, 47; limitations of, 46–47
American Civil Liberty Union, 44
America's Most Wanted, 7
analysis of sexual recidivism: bivariate, 59–62; regression, 63–69, 129n.6; studies, 21, 29, 62, 69, 123n.6, 124n.1
ATSA (Association for the Treatment of Sexual Abusers), 126n.6

Baltimore Sun, 47
Bowers v Hardwick, 41
Bureau of Justice Statistics, 9, 32, 33, 38, 43, 100, 111

Center for Disease Control and Prevention, 3
Center for Sex Offender Management, 8, 9, 10, 93, 99, 106
chemical castration, 27
community-based sanctions, 8–9, 10
community-based treatments and family, 125n.5
community notification; definition of, 5; implications of, 40–42; labeling issues, 43; legislation of, 37–40; problems of plea negotiations with, 42
Connecticut Department of Public Safety v John Doe, 39
containment approach of community supervision. *See* probation

cost-benefit analysis of crime. *See* deterrence

Davis, Richard Allen, 42
Depo-Provera. *See* chemical castration
deterrence, 13–18, 22, 72, 124n.13, 129n.3; and assessment of "costs," 28, 55, 57, 67–68, 72, 99, 101–103; legal repercussions, 101–102, 107; and legislation, 11, 109–110. *See also* rational choice theory
Doe v Poritz, 44

false sense of security, 43
federal sex offender registration, 38, 126n.6. *See also* registration of sex offenders
female sexual offenders, 13, 128n.1

gender and sex crimes, 32–33

Hagerman, Amber, 6, 44
Hendricks, Leroy, 42, 48–49
homophobia. *See* legislation of sex offending, as anti-gay sentiment

interview data: characteristics of respondents, 74–76; limitations, 73; protocol, 72; themes identified in, 77–94; types of offenses, 74
involuntary civil commitment: background of, 48–49, 126n.2; Constitution and, 126n.1; cost of, 51; dangerousness related to, 50; definition of, 47–48; policy limitations and, 114; typical procedures, 48; use of sexual predator language, 48